The core of success in schools is educator exper... ... words about how hard it can be but sheds sunlight onto evidence-based processes that lead to improvement. *Differentiated Supervision* asks for excellent diagnoses of teachers' needs, their theories of teaching, and the impact of current methods. Furthermore, it uses multiple coaching and supervision models to assist in the fidelity of implementation and provides processes for educators to work together to evaluate the impact on the learning lives of students. The book is rich in using feedback, look fors, and walkthroughs, as well as developing evaluative mind frames and equity checks—all leading to a bountiful harvest of student growth.

—John Hattie
Emeritus Laureate Professor, University of Melbourne
and Co-Director of the Hattie Family Foundation
Carlton, Victoria, Australia

In reconceptualizing supervision as a supporting process of continuous feedback, Mausbach and Morrison provide valuable insights into how school leaders can improve teaching and learning. This wonderfully written, comprehensive guide provides school leaders with the tools and strategies needed to strengthen collective efficacy and achieve improved results.

—Jenni Donohoo
Author/Education Consultant
New Orleans, LA

We differentiate instruction to meet the varied needs of students; why do we fail to do so for teachers? The authors have developed a model to remedy this, one that makes it possible for school leaders to provide the guidance and support all teachers deserve.

—Nancy Frey
Professor of Educational Leadership
San Diego State University
San Diego, CA

Differentiated Supervision

*This book is dedicated to all students and teachers
who love to learn and grow.*

Differentiated Supervision

Growing Teachers and Getting Results

Ann Mausbach

Kim Morrison

FOR INFORMATION:

Corwin

A SAGE Company

2455 Teller Road

Thousand Oaks, California 91320

(800) 233-9936

www.corwin.com

SAGE Publications Ltd.

1 Oliver's Yard

55 City Road

London, EC1Y 1SP

United Kingdom

SAGE Publications India Pvt. Ltd.

B 1/I 1 Mohan Cooperative Industrial Area

Mathura Road, New Delhi 110 044

India

SAGE Publications Asia-Pacific Pte. Ltd.

18 Cross Street #10-10/11/12

China Square Central

Singapore 048423

Printed in Canada.

Library of Congress Cataloging-in-Publication Data

Names: Mausbach, Ann T., author. | Morrison, Kimberly, author.

Title: Differentiated supervision : growing teachers and getting results/ Ann Mausbach, Kim Morrison.

Description: Thousand Oaks, California : Corwin Press, Inc., [2023] | Includes bibliographical references and index.

Identifiers: LCCN 2022011264 | ISBN 9781071853306 (paperback) | ISBN 9781071886816 (epub) | ISBN 9781071886823 (epub) | ISBN 9781071886830 (ebook)

Subjects: LCSH: School supervision. | School personnel management. | Teacher effectiveness. | Feedback (Psychology)

Classification: LCC LB2806.4 .M38 2023 | DDC 371.2/01–dc23/eng/ 20220617

LC record available at https://lccn.loc.gov/2022011264

President: Mike Soules

Vice President and Editorial Director: Monica Eckman

Senior Acquisitions Editor: Tanya Ghans

Content Development Manager: Desirée A. Bartlett

Editorial Assistant: Nyle De Leon

Production Editor: Tori Mirsadjadi

Copy Editor: Beth Ginter

Typesetter: Hurix Digital

Cover Designer: Scott Van Atta

Marketing Manager: Morgan Fox

This book is printed on acid-free paper.

FSC
www.fsc.org
MIX
Paper from
responsible sources
FSC® C103567

22 23 24 25 26 10 9 8 7 6 5 4 3 2 1

CONTENTS

LIST OF FIGURES

ACKNOWLEDGMENTS

We understand that the only way to help students improve is through working collaboratively. We have both been fortunate to work with groups of educators throughout our careers who have helped us evolve into stronger practitioners. There are too many to name here, but we want to thank all of the teachers and students who have helped shape our thinking.

We would also like to thank Tanya Ghans for her passion and dedication to making sure our message was clear and relevant to our readers. Her attention and advocacy have made the process so much richer for us. We would also like to thank Desirée Bartlett for her technical assistance.

Our families' roots have kept us grounded. Their love and support provide the light that helps us thrive. Thank you, Tim, Jack, Mark, Andre, Samantha, Max, and Leo.

PUBLISHER'S ACKNOWLEDGMENTS

Corwin gratefully acknowledges the contributions of the following reviewers:

Amanda E. Austin
Director, STEM Academy (Iberville Parish)
Addis, LA

Chestin Auzenne-Curl
Independent Consultant/Lecturer, Texas A&M University
Atascocita, TX

Ray Boyd
Principal, West Beechboro Independent Primary School
Beechboro, Australia

Mona Fairley-Nelson
Deputy Head of School, Carol Morgan School
Atlanta, GA

ABOUT THE AUTHORS

Ann Mausbach, coauthor of *Leading Student-Centered Coaching: Building Principal and Coach Partnerships* (Corwin, 2018), *School Leadership Through the Seasons: A Guide to Staying Focused and Getting Results All Year* (Routledge Eye on Education, 2016), and *Align the Design: A Blueprint for School Improvement* (ASCD, 2008), has been an educator for over 30 years. Ann's belief that the greatest investment a leader can make is in people not programs has focused her work on supporting principals and teacher leaders with the tools they need to align purpose with action. Her administrative experience includes serving as a coordinator of staff development, director of curriculum, director of elementary education, and an assistant superintendent for curriculum and instruction. She currently works as an associate professor for educational leadership at Creighton University in Omaha, Nebraska.

Kim Morrison, coauthor of *School Leadership Through the Seasons: A Guide to Staying Focused and Getting Results All Year* (Routledge Eye on Education, 2016), is the principal of an urban elementary school located in the Midwest. Her administrative experiences have included elementary, middle, and district administration for over 20 years. She has primarily worked in at-risk environments addressing complicated issues of equity, poverty, homelessness, and special education. She was named Middle School Principal of the Year by School Administrators of Iowa in 2016. She has been the coordinator for new teacher induction, McKinney Vento Homeless Grant, and Safe and Drug Free Schools.

INTRODUCTION

"Remember that children, marriages, and flower gardens reflect the kind of care they get."

H. Jackson Brown, Jr.

THE ROOTS OF DIFFERENTIATED SUPERVISION

Supervision—such a loaded word for many educators. For teachers, this means memories of hours spent nervously preparing lessons, hoping to fill the time with all the correct techniques so the principal can check all the correct boxes on an endless rubric, and then being agreeable during the post-observation conference so that the experience is over as soon as possible so they can get back to their classroom and teach in their "normal" way. For principals, it conjures up the stress of trying to fit in an inordinate number of observations in the last few frantic months of school, using cumbersome forms and then sharing generic feedback around broad and widely interpreted teaching standards. Lots of work for very little return for everybody.

Having been involved in both types of experiences, early on in our administrative careers (which now span over 20 plus years for each of us) we knew there had to be a better way to support teachers and positively impact the students in our care. Experience had taught us that if we messed with something like supervision it would have to be connected to our overall efforts in improving the school. Treating supervision as an isolated activity didn't work; we had gone down that path and knew it was a big waste of time for teachers and leaders and resulted in little impact for students.

We began revisioning a system for supervision based on the principle that schools are complex systems, meaning they are made up of multiple interconnected parts. The more tightly coupled the parts the more likely improvements to the system would be sustainable. The level of interdependency inherent in a garden helps explain this thinking. Change one aspect of a garden (i.e., type of fertilizer) and it impacts the whole garden, either positively or negatively. We also believe supervision is all about growth and not just about pulling weeds. Addressing ineffective supervision required us to dig at the roots of the issue because changes would impact the entire school. Hacking around at the dead branches wasn't enough; we needed a comprehensive framework. The differentiated supervision model is the response.

DIFFERENTIATED SUPERVISION DEFINED

Differentiated supervision is a comprehensive model that provides a coherent method for supporting individuals, small groups, and the whole school in implementing high-leverage strategies that improve student learning. The model is organized so that leaders can differentiate based on both teacher needs and supervision practices. Differentiation by teacher means knowing, understanding, and responding to the unique needs of individual teachers. No two teachers' needs are exactly the same, so supervision practices that treat them as such miss the mark. Feedback tools in the differentiated supervision model are designed to help leaders pinpoint areas of support for individual teachers. Processes provide structure but also allow for flexibility so if a teacher needs more support that can easily be accommodated.

Differentiation by process means using a variety of supervision methods to provide support to teachers. Multiple methods are needed to provide the leader with an in-depth understanding of the teachers' needs. A mixture of supervisory practices (i.e., general walkthroughs, implementation studies, etc.) will be shared throughout the book, not to purport one method over another, but in an effort to help leaders know when and how to use these practices in a manner that creates coherence rather than chaos. In essence, we will be sharing how to differentiate which practice will have the greatest impact in the context of the work you are doing both at the building and individual level.

Supervision is more than a series of steps that lead to a final evaluation. For us, as corny as this may sound, it is a way of being. It is about creating a culture where examining practice, working together to figure out issues, and constantly improving are the norms. Supervision is about supporting and directing, not judging and complying. Changing the culture and achievement in a school requires a broadened definition of supervision, one that moves away from thinking it is just about appraisal and viewing it as a powerful fertilizer for growth.

IT TAKES COMMITMENT

A commitment is a pledge or promise to the purpose of your enterprise. Making a commitment is crucial because it's what transforms words into reality. For those of us in schools, that means a commitment to learning. As we express and transmit commitments to those around us, it leads to the creation of new behaviors and attitudes (Daskal, 2016). When new experiences are provided that allow individuals to practice and build upon their learning, commitment increases. In other words, when we do the work, belief and dedication to change follow. This serves as a call to action for leaders. We must commit to doing this work by engaging in behaviors that will transform beliefs and ultimately the system, exactly what the differentiated supervision model is designed to do. Committing to the work of teaching and learning must be a deliberate process. Leaders have to be clear about what they want to sow, then do the work required to plant and nurture seeds of improvement.

We have found three core leadership commitments help focus a leader's attention and ensure that the differentiated supervision model gets implemented in an impactful way. These commitments flow from the components that make up the professional capital equation (Hargreaves & Fullan, 2012). These include human (individual talent), social (how groups work together and interact), and decisional (ability to make good decisions based on experience and learning) capital. Leading learning involves having all three capitals interact and work together to move the school forward. As you read the following chapters, we encourage you to reflect on how these commitments are manifested in the model.

CORE LEADERSHIP COMMITMENTS
Human: Use of a growth mindset to develop and enhance professional capital.
Social: Development of a school culture that promotes learning.
Decisional: Implementation of school improvement processes at high levels.

THE BOOK CHAPTERS

Building Level Focus

Element I
Universal Support
Qualitative Feedback
Process: Walkthroughs

Element III
Universal Support
Quantitative Feedback
Process:
Implementation Study

Formative

FEEDBACK

Summative

Element II
Individual/Small Group
Qualitative Feedback
Processes: Focused walkthroughs/PLCs

Element IV
Individual
Quantitative Feedback
Process: District or state evaluation process

Classroom Level Focus

DIFFERENTIATED SUPERVISION MODEL

The differentiated supervision model graphic outlined in Chapter 1 is the organizer for the book. Four quadrants are used to describe the major areas of supervision as well as to demonstrate the interconnectedness between all components. One quadrant of the model is described in each of the Chapters 2–4. Leadership moves that increase the likelihood for successful implementation are included for each quadrant. The focus for feedback and practical examples of what this feedback would sound like will also be a part of each chapter. A From the Field vignette is used throughout the book to help readers see how the four quadrants work together to create focus.

Our buildings weather the seasons when they are nurtured by principals who focus on growth and know how to support teachers and students in this pursuit. We dedicated the last chapter to those leadership behaviors that will help do just that. Teachers flourish when led by a respectfully relentless principal. Chapter 6 teases out the specific nuanced leadership behaviors needed that help leverage the positive trajectory of a school.

OUR INTENTIONS

In reading this book, we hope to expand your definition of supervision so you can see how impactful it can be when it is woven throughout your daily work. We also hope that you see how the processes and tools can create a community of learners, having a positive effect on both the culture and achievement in your school. In seeing the interrelatedness of this model, we believe you will not only be more efficient with your supervision but be better equipped to provide relevant and powerful feedback. While leading a school is never easy, our desire is that by reading this book you will not only be inspired but equipped to know you can make a difference. Finally, our ultimate intention is to help you support the teachers and students in your care so they grow beyond measure.

A FEW THINGS YOU SHOULD KNOW

Before embarking on a journey of differentiated supervision, we want to clarify a few terms that you will see throughout the book. Because these terms can mean different things to different people, we are sharing our definitions so that as you encounter them throughout your reading you will have a clear picture of what we are describing.

SCHOOL IMPROVEMENT PLAN (SIP)

A school improvement plan (SIP) is the North Star for this work. Imagine building a house and having workers show up and do whatever they want to do. This sounds crazy, because it is, and yet it is what we do to teachers when they work in schools without a well-articulated SIP. Builders' blueprints outline what the structure will look like when it is completed. This provides direction and guidance so that everyone involved knows and understands what is being built. Building a strong school is no different. The SIP serves this function for schools.

A SIP is a planning document that outlines goals, strategies, and objectives. Having a clear, collaboratively developed plan that aligns with the mission, vision, and needs of the school helps create a culture that allows everyone to thrive because it creates a shared sense of purpose and builds a continuous improvement mindset. The goal of the SIP is to affect change in the system so it is developed in response to achievement and cultural data. Developing a focused plan will be outlined in Chapter 1.

PROFESSIONAL DEVELOPMENT SYSTEMS

Learning is messy. It doesn't occur in a straight line that connects point A to point B. It's more like the two-step—one step forward, two steps back. In addition to not being linear, learners aren't all starting at the same place or from the same vantage points. Deep learning requires time, practice, and feedback (Campitelli & Gobert, 2011). Organizing meaningful professional learning for adults in a school is difficult, if not impossible, if we don't pay attention to these important factors. The differentiated supervision model addresses these issues by being strategic about planning for adult learning. This happens in two ways: first, by aligning learning content to the strategies in the SIP, and second, by organizing learning in such a way that provides teachers ample opportunities to learn in a variety of settings. This means providing some whole group learning (when the concept is new) and copious amounts of small group (via professional learning communities, or PLCs, or learning teams) and one-on-one learning (through feedback). Developing a comprehensive professional development plan, which is outlined in Chapter 2, ensures that both of these things will happen.

INFRASTRUCTURE

The first step in making this work happen is to build an infrastructure of support. We use the term infrastructure because it refers to the physical and organizational structures needed for the operation of an enterprise. The infrastructure is pivotal because it is what holds up the rest of the work. Much like a trellis in a garden provides support and direction for plants to grow, so does the way a leader organizes the work of the adults. Without upfront planning on what these structures will be, the hope of implementation dies on the vine. Because more than one infrastructure of support is needed, we will address this concept in each chapter, providing specifics about what needs to be in place in order to hold up the framework as related to the content in that chapter.

TIMING

The differentiated supervision model is designed as a recursive process that provides consistency and structure for the school leader. There is a rhythm to this work that is driven by the seasons of the school year. Leaders use the qualitative and quantitative data gathered throughout the year to make decisions and support teachers. Appendix A provides a suggested outline of what needs to occur as you move throughout the school year.

CHAPTER 1

....

DIFFERENTIATED SUPERVISION 101

"Successful gardeners know when to use a rake versus a hoe. School leaders must approach supervision in this same manner, understanding which tool will yield the best results."

What Keeps Us Up at Night: *Have you ever worked really hard as a leader to improve your school only to find at the end of the year that student results weren't what you hoped for? You were frequently in classrooms, designed powerful learning activities for your staff, and followed the district evaluation protocols. Why are the results not what you desired?*

Having great schools requires having great teachers. Helping teachers grow is job number one for school leaders who want to make a direct impact on student learning. This sounds simple enough, but schools are complex systems. Cultivating seeds of improvement in a school requires patient attention, requiring leaders to not only know effective supervision practices, but also know when they should be used so they have the greatest impact. School leaders must be well versed in the effective processes of school supervision if they want to help teachers grow.

WHAT SUPERVISION IS AND WHAT IT IS NOT

Understanding the nuances in supervision begins with recognizing the multiplicative role that it plays in schools. According to Marshall (2013) there are five core functions of supervision: appraisal, affirmation, improvement, housecleaning, and quality assurance. Supervision, unlike evaluation, is a process that is designed to help teachers improve outcomes for students. It isn't about checklists or forms or providing lengthy feedback to teachers. At its essence, supervision is about supporting students because when done right it helps teachers do the complex work of advancing student learning. Evaluation is an event that determines whether or not the supervision process has been successful. The differentiated model connects supervision and evaluation practices while also allowing the core functions of supervision to happen in a focused and purposeful way.

THE CHALLENGE

Two common issues derail the use of critical supervision routines. The first is the sheer number of staff that leaders are required to supervise. According to the National Council of Education Statistics 2016 data, the average public school enrollment is 528 students. If there is an average of 25 students per class, this equates to approximately 21 teachers per school. Even if a school has assistants, supervision numbers can be in the double digits. The second challenge is the diversity of expertise found in the typical school staff. Skill levels can vary dramatically based not only on years of experience, but also on the individual's willingness to learn and try new techniques.

Addressing these complexities requires a new approach to supervision. This approach must account for the variability found in school staff while helping leaders provide feedback that impacts student growth. This requires a framework that allows leaders to differentiate supervision practices, just like classroom teachers do to accommodate the varied needs of their students.

Note This: Differentiated supervision of personnel means that school leaders do things differently based on what teachers need and students deserve (Mooney & Mausbach, 2008).

Differentiated supervision embraces a philosophy that is designed to match the level of supervision with the needs of both the individuals and teams while moving the entire school forward. Ongoing meaningful feedback serves as the centerpiece for this approach so teachers and leaders can work together to develop a mutual understanding about what students need to succeed.

The remainder of this chapter will serve as the first step in answering this challenge by introducing the fundamental elements of differentiated instruction. Then it will move into illustrating a model for differentiated supervision followed by the research on why this model is effective, and finally how to begin putting it into practice.

FIGURE 1.1 DIFFERENTIATED SUPERVISION MODEL

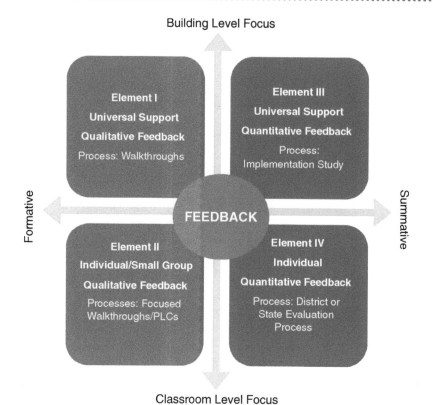

A MODEL FOR IMPROVED SUPERVISION

This model is not a recipe for how to approach supervision. We don't believe such a thing exists, and even if it did, we know that wouldn't work. Supervision requires a more nuanced approach. Nuanced leaders, according to Fullan (2019), have to comprehend the inner workings and see the patterns in order to understand how something works. Effective supervision requires moving beyond the simplistic notion that walk-throughs coupled with a comprehensive summative evaluation is enough. Both practices are needed and have their place; what matters most, however, is how these practices work together in the service of student learning.

Two Scopes: Focus and Assessment

The differentiated supervision model is built around two axes as illustrated in Figure 1.1. The model was designed around these axes in order to address the inherent challenge of improving an entire system while simultaneously addressing the individual needs of a diverse teaching staff. The two axes define the dimensions of differentiated supervision by intended focus (building or classroom) and the type of assessment (formative or summative).

The elements on the left-hand side of the matrix are where leaders should spend the majority of their day throughout the school year in terms of supervision. The descriptive nature of qualitative feedback used in these two elements generates ongoing information that helps teachers continually refine their practice. This formative data is vital to helping support teachers and will be the most significant factor in their growth and development.

Driven by Feedback

At the core of the differentiated supervision model is feedback. Feedback occupies this spot because it is central to how we learn and grow. Essentially, feedback is the information that we receive that helps to shape our next response (Nottingham & Nottingham, 2017). We agree wholeheartedly with Bambrick-Santoyo (2012) that "the primary purpose of observing teachers isn't to judge the teacher, but to find the most effective ways to coach them to improve student learning" (p. 63). This requires an approach to feedback that has teachers actively engaged so *they* can identify what is working and what they could do better next time.

Figure 1.2 depicts the frequency and tools for generating feedback in the differentiated supervision model. The school improvement and professional development plan serves as the lens for feedback as it provides the school with focus. Look fors act as the magnifying glass, allowing the teacher and leader to focus on specific well-defined practices. The intent of this model is to utilize feedback that promotes self-awareness, serving as that voice in a person's head that has them constantly thinking and reflecting on how to advance or change their performance. This is impossible if the feedback used is too generic or all encompassing. Science and experience have taught us that it is impossible to try to improve too many things at once. This is why the model relies heavily on collaboratively defined looks (see Chapter 2) because they lead to actionable feedback.

Feedback aligned to look fors helps identify areas for growth and provides specificity on how to move forward. The feedback techniques described throughout the book showcase how to promote reflection and dialogue, essential practices if we want supervision to be something teachers engage in rather than being done to them. Because state and district teaching standards tend to be broad and generic, they are typically used at the conclusion of observation cycles. Frequent feedback based on look fors generated from the school improvement and professional

FIGURE 1.2 FEEDBACK TIMING

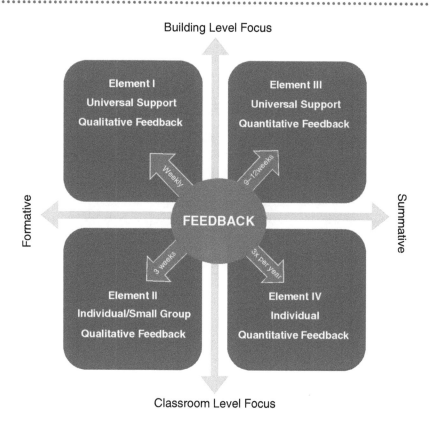

development plan, given in small relevant chunks over time, is at the heart of this model.

The Elements

The essence of this model is found in each of the four elements. While each element is distinct in both the supervision processes employed and the feedback content focus, it is the synergy of these elements, working in tandem with each other, that results in strong outcomes for students. An overview of each element can be found here, but each element will be the subject of a separate chapter.

Element I: Universal Support, Qualitative Feedback. Practices and processes in this element are designed to help move the school forward by providing focused feedback around the school improvement plan. In this first stage, principals, teachers, and other key leaders in the building work together to collaboratively define the focus for observation used during daily walk-throughs. We refer to these as "look fors," and they provide the basis for feedback.

Element II: Individual/Small Group Support, Qualitative Feedback. Practices in this element are targeted at individual teachers and small groups. While all elements are needed, this element packs a big punch in terms of affecting student achievement because it uses frequent observations in both classrooms and PLCs to provide targeted ongoing feedback.

Element III: Universal Support, Quantitative Feedback. Practices in this element are designed to help determine levels of implementation of school improvement plan efforts. This summative check is necessary in order to help identify what additional supports are needed so that all students benefit from improvement efforts.

Element IV: Individual Support, Quantitative Feedback. Practices in this element provide individuals with summative feedback on their overall teaching efforts. Methods in this element are dictated by state or district mandates. Feedback is based on teaching standards.

Supervision Practices

The differentiated supervision model hinges on using a range of supervision methods to provide support to teachers. While we are strong advocates for principals engaging in walkthroughs with feedback, that process alone won't help provide a leader with the big picture needed to help all staff and students grow. Figure 1.3 provides an outline of the differentiated practices that leaders need to use. Each practice will be explored in-depth in the corresponding element chapters. What is central to remember here is that all of these practices are necessary. What the differentiated supervision model does is help leaders determine when to use a specific practice so results can be leveraged. Successful gardeners know when to use a rake versus a hoe. School leaders must approach supervision in this same manner, understanding which tool will yield the best results.

WHY IT WORKS

Connecting Supervision to the System

The work of improving a school or district requires a system approach.

> **Note This: Systems that build a common language and knowledge base along with implementing proven effective practices outperform schools that do not have this focus (Robinson, 2011).**

The differentiated model works because it connects supervision to the rest of the system. Rather than treating supervision as an isolated activity that happens 3 times a year (or less) and is prescribed by forms, differentiated supervision is dictated by teacher needs and improvement strategies. Supervision becomes a supporting process in helping translate

FIGURE 1.3 DIFFERENTIATED SUPERVISION PRACTICES

PRACTICE	DESCRIPTION	PURPOSE	FREQUENCY/ DURATION	FEEDBACK METHOD	FEEDBACK COLLECTION TOOL
Element I General Walkthrough	Organized visit through a school's learning areas, using specific look fors to focus on teaching and learning	Identify building-wide trends and patterns regarding implementation of SIP in order to help determine "next steps" for professional development (PD)	Weekly, 3–5 minutes in each classroom	Face-to-face Schoolwide via blog, email, etc.	Feedback Log and Walkthrough Summary
Element II Focused Walkthrough	Observe teaching and learning in a specific grade level or content area	Learn instructional strengths and needs of individual teachers Follow up on learning from PLC	Depends on work in small group PD, but on average each teacher every 2–3 weeks, 10–20 minutes per class	Face-to-face email/note	Feedback Log and Walkthrough Summary
Element II Participation in PLCs	Weekly attendance at PLC meetings in order to serve as an active team member	Play an active role in helping support teachers as they analyze student work and plan to meet the needs of all students	Attendance once a week per team for 30 minutes	Small group during meetings	Feedback Log
Element III Implementation Study	Scheduled visits to measure quantitative data on SIP implementation	Determine how near or far the school is from reaching 100% implementation of strategies in SIP	Approximately 2–3x per year, may take 3 weeks to complete depending on building size	Schoolwide face-to-face	Feedback Log and Teacher Map
Element VI Formal Evaluation	Process outlined by the school or district used to judge whether or not the teacher can continue to work at the school	Determine teacher competency	Annually or more frequently based on the needs of the teacher	Individualized	Feedback Log, Teacher Map, and Walkthrough Summary

the vision of the organization into a reality by setting a direction that results in whole school consistency and high expectations, one of the core functions of system leadership (Leithwood, Day, Sammons, Harris, & Hopkins, 2006).

Figure 1.4 illustrates the role supervision plays in the blueprint processes for school improvement (Mooney & Mausbach, 2008). The five core processes include the following:

1. Establishing a mission, vision, and values that guide the general direction of the school and its future actions;

2. Using data analysis, which includes both collecting and interpreting data for decision-making;

3. Using a school improvement plan to guide goals, strategies, action steps, and decisions in order to create a working plan for the school;

4. Implementing professional development that serves as the engine for the school improvement plan; and

5. Differentiating supervision of teaching and learning to monitor how processes are working in classrooms.

When supervision is aligned to the other school improvement processes (mission and vision, data, the plan, and professional development), it helps to gauge progress and serves as the GPS of school improvement.

Supervision helps keep the plan safely on the road, preventing detours and helping determine when pit stops are needed. For example, if a strategy in the school improvement plan is implementing project-based learning, then the professional development should focus on helping teachers use project-based learning. Individual professional growth plans would then include teachers identifying aspects of project-based learning that they are going to focus on throughout the year to improve their practice. Supervision is where the real work of implementing the school improvement plan happens. Without supervision the plan becomes another misguided initiative.

Note This: The school improvement plan is the road map and professional development is the engine, but it is supervision that provides guidance on how near or far a school is from the targets.

Capacity Building Through Formative and Summative Practices

The research is clear that developing capacity is of central importance to school leaders (Fullan & Quinn, 2016). Collective capacity building works because it involves deepening staff know-how through knowledge

FIGURE 1.4 BLUEPRINT PROCESSES FOR SCHOOL IMPROVEMENT

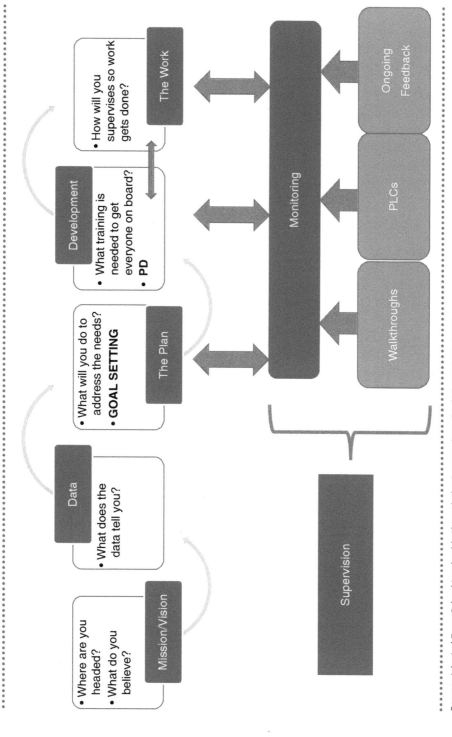

Source: Adapted From *School Leadership Through the Seasons* (Mausbach & Morrison, 2016).

building, collective action, and consistent focus. The goal of collective capacity building is for everyone in the system to have the necessary knowledge and skills. This requires attention to both individual and collective growth. Like the gardener who has one eye on individual plant growth and the other on the overall harvest, leaders must use both formative and summative practices to determine how deep the roots of learning have been planted.

The differentiated supervision model hinges on the use of both formative and summative measures. Formative measures use frequent monitoring so leaders can address learning differences in order to lessen the knowing–doing gap. Summative measures help leaders in assessing what has been accomplished and aid in helping to make decisions on where to go next. Both are critical to creating communities of learners.

Human and Social Capital Are Interconnected

The notion that a singular heroic leader is needed to improve a system has been replaced by the understanding that it takes a team (think Avengers rather than Superman). The team is more powerful than the individual. This doesn't discount that individuals matter—the quality of the teacher and leader in a school has been well established as a major influence on student achievement (Leithwood et al., 2006; Marzano, 2003). However, if leaders want to improve teacher quality (human capital), leveraging the quality of groups (social capital) accelerates this process (Hargreaves & Fullan, 2012). Individuals develop capacity when they are learning and getting feedback from the powerful interactions and relationships around them. The work of developing human capital flows from the skills and knowledge developed through collaborative learning experiences. Human and social capital are intertwined much like a plant is to soil. Plants can grow without soil, but place them in the ground and surround them with the right conditions (water, fertilizer, other healthy plants) and they thrive. Social capital is the soil for improvement. It is more powerful than human capital, but the two feed off of each other (Fullan & Quinn, 2016). Individuals flourish when we root them in rich and meaningful experiences with their colleagues.

The differentiated supervision model is predicated on the symbiotic relationship between human, social, and decisional (discussed in Chapter 4) capital. In this model, the learning that occurs during collaborative work serves as a lens for helping determine how to support individual teachers. Individual skill and knowledge development are complemented by group learning. Group work, when done right, serves as the platform for deep learning, allowing individuals to collaboratively wrestle with the complexities of helping all students learn and in turn improving individual performance. Emphasis is placed on the practices on the right side of the matrix so we can as Fullan (2019) says, "use the group to change the group" (p. 79). Rather than spending inordinate amounts of time trying to improve one teacher at a time and seeing slow or incremental gains, this model requires leaders to shift more attention to group dynamics. Strategizing about who should work together and how they should work is a central focus of the leader in the differentiated supervision model.

MAKING IT HAPPEN

The coherent use of school improvement processes provides the foundation for the differentiated supervision model. Developing a rich understanding of how to connect supervision to school improvement efforts is job number one for principals. Armed with this understanding, the principal can then work to make sure that improvement efforts are focused and result in deep levels of implementation that positively impact student outcomes. The leadership practices outlined in the next section provide practical guidance on how to make this happen.

Build the Infrastructure: Create Feedback Cycles

In the wise words of Miles Davis, "Time isn't the main thing, it is the only thing." Simply put, if you don't build time into your calendar, this work will never get done. Supervising teaching and learning can't be an afterthought. The only way we have found to make this happen is by committing to the time in the leader's schedule every week of the school year. Four important tasks must be designated in the principal's weekly calendar: providing weekly feedback to the entire staff via a weekly message, participating in PLCs, observing in teachers' classrooms, and providing face-to-face feedback. This can seem overwhelming without a strategic approach to attacking the work. Strategies for making this happen will be addressed in the latter part of the chapter.

Developing a rotating schedule that divides staff into three feedback cycle groups is one such technique. Using three groups provides the principal with a manageable way to see all staff on a consistent basis while still providing time to attend to the other unplanned events that pop up regularly in a school day. Cycles also ensure that every teacher will have face-to-face feedback once in a 3-week time period. Building sizes vary, but we have found that a 3-week cycle is manageable for mid- to large-size schools. Two feedback cycles could be used with a smaller staff, or if there are multiple administrators, this would increase frequency of observations and feedback. The minimum expectation is face-to-face feedback every 3 weeks. The only caveat to this is first-year teachers who, at least for the first semester, are observed every week.

In off-cycle weeks, teachers still receive feedback via the weekly message and in PLCs. Using collaboratively defined look fors makes this feedback

FIGURE 1.5 TEACHER FEEDBACK

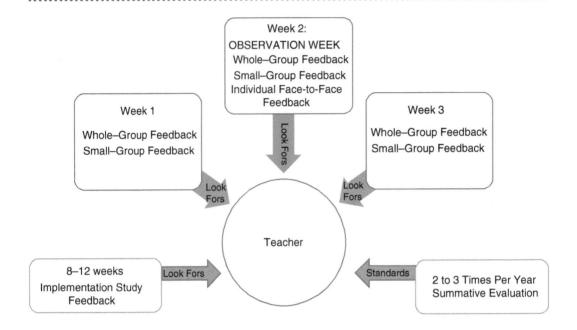

relevant and useful, promoting consistency across the school. Figure 1.5 depicts how much feedback a teacher receives in the differentiated supervision model. Weeks 1–3 are from the formative side of the matrix, while the lower boxes are from the summative side.

We are ardent believers of creating a schedule for this work, however, who gets observed may need to change due to what has been observed and the work of PLCs. For example, you may observe in a PLC that one teacher's student data is much lower than the other teacher's student data in the grade level or subject area so the frequency of observation is increased to every week or every 2 weeks. This is much easier to do when time slots are blocked out each week for this work. In other words, create the schedule, but *differentiate* based on teacher needs.

Align School Improvement Processes

Alignment of school improvement is when all the processes (mission and vision, data, the plan, professional development, and supervision) work in concert (Mooney & Mausbach, 2008). It is the interconnectedness of these processes that determine the success of the school (see Figure 1.4). Gardens grow when all facets are interacting and working together. The same holds true for schools: If one of the core processes is missing, improvement is hindered. The key for leaders is to align the processes and help connect the dots for teachers.

Alignment happens when the leader has the mindset that everything in the organization is instrumental to the achievement of collective goals. Rather than spending time looking for the latest quick fix to use as the improvement lever, leaders look within to align the processes and resources in a systematic and focused way (Elmore, 2008). Using the mission to guide what data to collect, identifying professional development practices based on the strategies in the school improvement plan, and using look fors to determine what to observe in classrooms are examples of how these processes help leaders look from within. Each process requires the leader to collaborate with staff to make decisions about the direction of the school. Decisions made throughout the cycle of school improvement lay the groundwork for developing collective commitments that directly impact how staff works together.

Many times, schools and districts believe they have alignment because they have several of these processes in place. For example, a mission statement may exist, and schools may have improvement plans and engage in data analysis. However, these processes are done in isolation of each other and are treated as separate activities rather than as actions that must interosculate in order to get maximum results. Misalignment is so detrimental because it perpetuates the "silo" mentality that is far too rampant in many schools. Silos get created because there isn't a shared sense of purpose on what and how to do the work. Breaking these silos down requires leaders to take alignment issues head-on so staff can find their footing in the improvement journey. Figure 1.6 outlines some common problems with alignment and actions leaders can take to address these problems.

FIGURE 1.6 COMMON ALIGNMENT PROBLEMS AND SOLUTIONS

PROBLEM	PRINCIPAL ACTIONS TO ADDRESS
Addressing mission and vision only at the beginning of each school year	• Frequently refer to the mission and vision when engaging in school improvement work • Highlight examples of the mission in action throughout the year • Use the mission as a touchstone when making decisions
Using annual data analysis vs. continuous data analysis for decision-making	• Distribute data as it becomes available followed by analysis and collective interpretation • Clearly identify data points in the school improvement plan that help measure impact on student learning and then collect this data on an ongoing basis and share progress with staff • Establish collaboration, such as PLCs, that use student data as the cornerstone for the work

(Continued)

FIGURE 1.6 (Continued)

Treating development of a school improvement plan as a one-time event driven by compliance with an outside source (i.e., district office, accreditation agency)	• Use school data to determine areas for improvement • Identify both implementation and impact data points, collect on an ongoing basis and revise plan as needed throughout the year
Developing professional development plans based on outside influences Creating professional development plans that are loosely related to the school improvement plan	• Develop professional development around identified needs of the school from the school improvement plan • Actively participate in PD and PLCs • Create an infrastructure for learning in the school that promotes both large and small group learning • Resist trainings, programs, or initiatives that are not a part of the strategies in the school improvement plan
Supervising teachers using daily monitoring methods that are not connected to the school improvement or professional development plan	• Set clear expectations regarding frequent classroom visitation for the purpose of monitoring teaching and learning in addition to evaluation of teachers • Collaboratively develop clear look fors around the school's initiatives so everyone understands what implementation looks like and sounds like

Source: Adapted from *Align the Design* (Mooney & Mausbach, 2008).

Alignment is a key factor in maximizing supervision efforts because it helps to create a shared ethos. It promotes the "we are all in this together" mentality since everyone is working toward the same desired state. An aligned system actualizes a growth mindset since it is built upon the notion of continuous improvement. When alignment is present, getting better at what we do becomes a part of the daily routine of the school. Learning from each other to meet collective goals is a common practice. Feedback is sought after and used. Supervision is no longer an unwanted, unsolicited intrusion from higher-ups but a helpful process that promotes growth.

Be Relentless About Focus and Clarity

Large-scale improvement doesn't happen without a tight instructional focus sustained over time (Elmore, 2008). Focus happens when what is of essential importance in the context of the organization is identified and efforts are concentrated on these essentials. However, the complex nature of schools often finds leaders caught in a frustrating game of whack a mole, trying to lead multiple initiatives all at once. While this game keeps a leader busy, it leaves them (and those they lead) tired and curious when results haven't improved. A lack of focus has the same catastrophic results as the garden that isn't weeded. Competing initiatives vie for teachers' time and attention and result in frantic activity that leads nowhere.

Achieving a laser-like focus requires leaders to boil down change into the smallest number of key high-yield strategies that have an impact on learning, also known as Fullan's notion of "skinny" (2009). This is difficult to do in a complex system like a school. Getting skinny requires schools to take a ruthless look at reality and then make hard decisions about what should and shouldn't be pursued. The school improvement and professional development plan serves as the tool for this work because it promotes decision-making and links goals with action. This plan can provide clarity and coherence, but only when the following key practices are utilized.

Use Clear and Deliberate Language

Schools and school systems are highly compartmentalized both by physical and organizational design. Teachers in the science wing may rarely interact with the fine arts wing, not only because they are physically separated, but because the school schedule does not allow for common planning or lunch times. This isolation hampers reform efforts and adds to confusion or disengagement, complicating supervision efforts. Because this isolation exists, it is important to use common language so that everyone is on the same page. Figure 1.7 outlines questions and language that create shared meaning and clarity across a school staff. Using common language assists with staff knowing what is being built and how near or far the collective team is from reaching targets.

FIGURE 1.7 QUESTIONS AND LANGUAGE FOR DEVELOPING A SCHOOL IMPROVEMENT PLAN

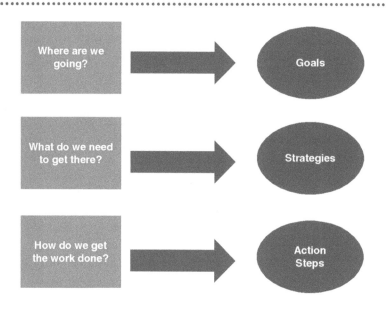

Limit the Number of Goals and Strategies

Setting clear goals and then coordinating the work of the adults around that is how focus happens. Goal setting forces leaders to determine what is most important given all the important things that need to get done (Robinson, 2018). If the purpose of having goals is to determine direction, then having five or more goals means five or more destinations, putting the school on divergent paths. One useful way to help limit goals is to keep them centered on student outcomes. Then strategies are about the work of the adults to help meet the goal. For example, one goal area may be to improve achievement. Under this goal, there may be two strategies such as to implement formative assessments and improve feedback practices to students. On the surface, these goals and strategies seem simple; it is in the execution that complexity enters the picture. This is why it is essential to limit it to a manageable number.

Remember Programs Aren't Strategies

Strategies operationalize the goal, and in order for the goal to be met by all students, all staff need to clearly understand what needs to be accomplished. A clearly articulated strategy aids in staff's understanding of the work that lies ahead. Identifying a program as a strategy undermines supervision and continuous improvement efforts because it communicates that meeting the goal is outside of the teacher's influence and all that is necessary is to purchase and implement. While there are many good resources and programs available to teachers, what matters most is the quality of the teacher (Marzano, Pickering, & Pollock, 2001). Commercially developed programs are effective when they are placed in the hands of a competent teacher who knows not only how to use the tool, but why and for which students. Rather than focusing a strategy on a program, a school leader is better served by focusing on people and process, which is the essence of the differentiated supervision model. The practices in the model account for the differences in staff competency and provide a process for supporting teachers in their practice.

Use Professional Development Needs as the Barometer

The best indicator as to whether or not the goals, strategies, and action steps in the school improvement plan are doable is to take a close look at the professional learning needs that stem from the plan. Listing all of the things teachers would need to know and be able to do if the strategies were implemented by the entire staff provides a realistic picture of the likelihood of the success of the plan. If the plan requires teachers to learn a long list of new practices, then the plan is too big. Can every single teacher in the school take on everything that is listed? Too often that answer is no, so scale back. Many times, we confuse staff lack of implementation of new strategies as a reluctance to change when in reality it may just be that we have asked staff to do too much changing and they don't know where to start. Just as the barometric meter alerts us about changes in weather conditions so we can react appropriately, the amount of professional learning required in plans serves as an indicator of the reasonableness of improvement efforts. It alerts us to whether there will be stormy times ahead (asking teachers to learn too many new things at once) or sunny days (giving teachers the time and space to learn a limited number of high leverage practices).

EQUITY CHECK

Differentiation at its essence is the act of recognizing the distinctions in and between things. Without a noticing of differences, uniqueness can't be valued and enhanced in a way that is responsive and affirming. The differentiated supervision model recognizes, values, and supports teachers in a way that accounts for diversity in their learning so they can address differences they find in student learning. Inherent to the model is providing all teachers with *what they need* so they can effectively support their students.

A focus on high expectations and high support for everyone dismantles the lottery approach to supervision where only a few students are lucky enough to land in an effective teacher's classroom. This approach upends an inequitable system by designing processes that meet people where they are and provides footholds to get to the next level. Using the practices in this model helps shape the leaders' thinking and actions on equity so the mission of teaching *all* students can finally be realized.

FROM THE FIELD

At Issue: Gail was a principal. She had a large staff and knew that in order to move the achievement needle she would have to have all staff working with the same focus. Although she worked hard during the first year at the school, the student results weren't what she desired. Determined to change things, Gail took a different approach to her supervision. Using the differentiated model as her guide, she connected her work to the school improvement plan.

Gail started her journey at the school by making sure she made time for the things that mattered most: teacher collaboration and spending time in classrooms. She developed a schedule that had teams collaborating on a weekly basis and administrators attending PLCs and conducting daily classroom observations. In addition to carving out time for teacher teams, Gail also designated time each week to coordinate feedback efforts with her leadership team which consisted of two assistant principals. Developing a schedule that devoted time to observing and collaborating with teachers before the year started ensured this work was a priority for Gail and her leadership team.

Once the collaboration schedule was in place, Gail and her staff worked to develop a focused school improvement plan. After reviewing data, they identified goals around student achievement. The strategy of writing and implementing learning intentions and success criteria was identified as the means to help them meet their targeted goals. Professional development around learning intentions and success criteria helped staff understand expectations. A collaborative process was used to develop look fors that helped staff understand what the strategy would look like and sound like when implemented in classrooms.

Element I. Once look fors were firmly in place, Principal Gail monitored the effectiveness of the school improvement plan. Gail made sure to visit classrooms every week and provided feedback based on the look fors via her weekly message. She used a weekly blog to highlight practices she observed that matched the look fors. Whole group professional development sessions provided teachers with rich learning on how to develop and use learning intentions and success criteria. Insights from general walkthroughs conducted each week informed this professional development.

Element II. Through her general walkthrough, Gail noticed that a team of teachers needed additional support. The teachers had strong instructional skills and were conscientious in their planning and collaborative practice. However, achievement was low, and students were not reaching growth targets. She knew she needed to spend more time with this team and became the lead learner with the teachers in studying the grade-level standards and planning authentic experiences for students. She worked with this team to unpack standards and to write quality learning intentions with specific success criteria. Together they would "do the student work" so they could put themselves in the shoes of the students. This work, coupled with focused walkthroughs and feedback, resulted in teachers using more explicit language that helped them differentiate based on student needs.

Element III. Implementation studies were conducted every 8 weeks to measure the percentage of teachers effectively utilizing success criteria and learning intentions, the strategy from the school improvement plan. The implementation study involved Gail and the assistants observing in every classroom and indicating whether the look fors were present or not. This qualitative data provided the leadership team with the percentage of teachers implementing the strategy. Teachers knew that the goal of 100% implementation with 80% fidelity was the bar to reach.

Element IV. Throughout the year, Gail collected the feedback given to the teachers from all of the elements. Conducting summative evaluations was simplified because she had a multitude of data at her fingertips. Conferences with teachers connected to the state's teaching standards and used authentic evidence to support areas of strength and areas for growth. Teachers found value in these conversations because they provided a summary of the work the teacher had done all year and didn't rely on irrelevant measures.

The process was focused and driven by feedback. The differentiated supervision approach worked for Gail and her team as student results and teacher job satisfaction soared.

 ## Key Takeaways

Leadership is complicated work that requires consistent attention to what drives growth. Creating conditions for growth necessitates a focus on what teachers know and can do both individually and collectively. It requires a framework that helps the leader simultaneously tend to the needs of the building, the team, and the individual teacher. The differentiated supervision model does this by helping the leader organize practices in a purposeful way so growth is realized throughout the school. The processes and tools used in each element of the differentiated supervision model help ensure coherence across the system.

Schools, like gardens, can be chaotic and wild—the soil, untilled and dormant. The differentiated model alleviates the distractions and noise around school improvement and supervision, cultivating a focused culture of collective action based on teacher and student needs. Leaders tame the chaos by targeting a small number of school improvement strategies, providing consistent feedback, and differentiating how they support teams and individuals—the fundamental constructs of the differentiated supervision model. The results are a bountiful harvest of improved achievement for all.

WHERE ARE YOU NOW?

Successfully implementing the differentiated supervision model requires a leader to commit to capacity building. Capacity, according to Fullan and Quinn (2016), "refers to the capability of the individual or organization to make the changes required and involves the development of knowledge, skills, and commitments" (pp. 56–57). This is of critical importance because every action a leader takes, either intentional or unintentional, reverberates throughout the school. Without a leader's commitment to learning and action, it is difficult if not impossible to create a culture of growth, which is a hinge point of the differentiated supervision model.

Building capacity calls for serious and intentional focus on helping others develop their talents through the process of developing your own. A garden can't thrive without a skilled gardener orchestrating the work. The same holds true for schools. This doesn't mean that the principal has to be -all-knowing, we know that doesn't work. What it does mean is that the principal has to be the "lead learner" organizing the work so that collaboratively, teams can improve student learning. And this necessitates attention to specific knowledge, skills, and follow through on the part of the leader. As we work through the differentiated supervision model, we have provided an inventory of what this entails. Chapters 1–5 will include a self-assessment designed to help you think and reflect so you can identify areas of strength and pinpoint areas where capacity building needs more attention.

Use the following continuum to rate yourself on each of the statements. Ask yourself what you need to change or do to move down the continuum toward blooming.

Getting started

Practices firmly in place

Planting seeds

Blooming

Knowledge	I understand the importance of connecting the processes of school improvement (mission and vision, data, the plan, professional development, and supervision) and continually work toward alignment.
	I am clear about the difference between supervision and evaluation.
	I understand how actionable feedback is necessary to drive my school improvement plan.
	I realize that formative and summative measures are needed to provide a complete picture of a teacher's performance.
Skills	A clear and focused school improvement plan (limited goals and clear language) has been developed collaboratively with staff.
	All staff are able to articulate the goals and strategies in the school improvement plan.
Follow Through	I have developed and am using a clear system in place for how I organize my days and weeks that allows me to observe teachers and attend PLC meetings.
	Cycles for observations and feedback have been developed.

CHAPTER 2

....

ELEMENT I
Universal Support With Qualitative Feedback

"A gardener isn't satisfied when only a few plants bloom and neither should the school leader be when only a handful of teachers are effective."

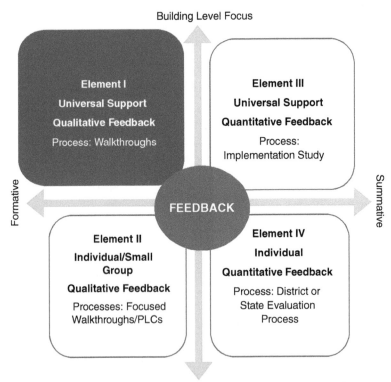

What Keeps Us Up at Night: Have you ever felt overwhelmed with how much improvement your school needs to make? You spent a lot of time with your staff developing a school improvement plan and now wonder how to put it into action? How do the practices get operationalized so student achievement is impacted? How do you help all staff feel a unity of purpose?

The research is clear. When schools organize themselves around a small number of shared goals and work collectively toward those goals, teachers will see a dramatic increase in student achievement (Elmore, 2004; Fullan, 2014). This sounds simple, but in reality, it can be extremely challenging, especially if a leader has the wrong mindset regarding supervision. A gardener isn't satisfied when only a few plants bloom and neither should the school leader be when only a handful of teachers are effective. Achieving a bountiful harvest requires attention to the entire system. *All* individuals in the system must develop a shared depth of understanding about the purpose and nature of teaching and learning, what Fullan and Quinn (2016) call coherence. To put it another way, schools aren't going to improve if efforts are focused on "fixing" one teacher at a time.

Coherence is a natural byproduct of differentiated supervision. This is because central to this model is alignment of supervision to a clearly articulated school improvement and professional development plan. These processes allow leaders and their teams to identify what is most important and concentrate all efforts on these essentials. The practices in Element I help leaders shift the focus of their observations from broad generic standards or practices to focusing on specific feedback aligned to schoolwide goals and strategies.

CLARIFYING THE MODEL

Focus: School

The focus in this element is monitoring how the school is improving overall, so the primary process used is the general walkthrough. The general walkthrough is an organized unannounced visit through the school's learning areas to observe teaching and learning, specifically the strategies outlined in the school improvement plan. The general walkthrough allows the leader to observe whether or not professional learning is being implemented and more importantly if it is making a difference for students. The general walkthrough, when used as described here, provides formative data that helps the leader determine next steps in the improvement journey.

The general walkthrough we recommend has four fundamental steps that distinguish this process from other methods: focus, look & talk, reflection, and feedback.

> *Look fors are clear statements that describe an observable teaching or learning behavior, strategy, outcome, product, or procedures (Mooney & Mausbach, 2008).*

Focus: Before a leader sets foot in a classroom to conduct a general walkthrough, there needs to be a shared understanding of expectations. Both the teachers and leaders require a common language and agreed-upon definitions for walkthroughs to be effective. Therefore, collaboratively developing look fors aligned to the school improvement plan is the first step.

The use of look fors assists teachers and administrators in focusing on specific teaching and learning aspects. They bridge the gap between learning and implementation because they help teachers understand the target. A more detailed discussion on look fors can be found later in this chapter.

Look & Talk: Once the look fors are firmly in place, the leader needs to let the staff know which ones are the focus of the walkthrough and then set out and spend 5–10 minutes in the classrooms. Two critical practices characterize the general walkthrough. The first is reviewing samples of student work posted in hallways and work folders. The second practice is to talk to students. One of the main purposes of the general walkthrough is to ensure that the strategies in the school improvement plan are being implemented at high levels *and* are resulting in changes in student achievement. Examining student work and talking to students is the only way to determine effectiveness. Hattie's (2009) mantra "know thy impact" is central to this process. The focal point of these observations is to look for learning.

Looking at the outputs (student learning) rather than inputs (teacher behavior) makes this a student-centered process and is more palatable to teachers. Because the general walkthrough is not an announced visit, it is difficult to hit every classroom at that exact moment when the teacher is engaged in using the strategies, so it is imperative to take time to talk to students and examine work. Gardeners know the plants are growing by examining the plants, we have to do the same in schools. We have to talk to our students and look at their work. Common questions to ask students when in classrooms include the following:

- What did you learn by completing this assignment that you didn't know before?

- What does your teacher want you to learn by doing this lesson?

- What have you learned this year that is helping you be a better reader or writer?

- How does this lesson connect to what you learned yesterday?

- How do you know when you have done quality work?

Reflect: Once the walkthrough is complete, the principal needs to take time to reflect on what was seen. A busy principal rarely has time to do this immediately after completing a general walkthrough, so it is recommended to have some method of collecting information from the visit. It is easy to voice record on a smartphone what was observed or use the timeless note-paper on a clipboard. The key is to document enough information so that rich reflection can occur. (We describe one method, the feedback log, later in this chapter.) During reflection the principal needs to be able to identify what was observed that "hit the mark" (matched the look fors), determine how many classrooms demonstrated the look fors, and identify next steps by looking at trends and patterns across classrooms.

Be Wary of Checklists for Element I

We do not advocate using checklists as a documentation method in this element. Checklists promote compliance as they are focused on whether or not the practice is present; they can't discern whether or not the practice will make a difference, nor do they lend themselves to effective feedback. When Ann's boys were taking driver's education, they had a 16-point checklist they needed to complete before starting the car. While this helped them get the car started properly, it was no guarantee that they would be able to navigate the roads success-fully. A checklist may be useful in Element III, but due to focus on qualitative feedback, look fors are the better tool. Figure 2.1 outlines the difference between checklists and look fors.

FIGURE 2.1 DIFFERENCE BETWEEN CHECKLISTS AND LOOK FORS

	CHECKLIST	LOOK FORS
Purpose	To determine whether or not a step or concept is in place	Clearly state in observable terms what the teaching practice, process, behavior, and strategy look like and sound like when implemented so that teachers develop a shared understanding
Development	Typically focus on a generic set of instructional practices	Look fors are based on the school improvement and professional development plan, and are developed collaboratively after a staff has engaged in learning
Feedback Focus	Focused on quantifiable results, such as whether or not the item was observed or present	Validates practice through describing what was observed that matched look fors and why that matters, also promotes reflection
Example of Feedback	"When I observed in your class today, 7 out of 10 students were completing the task assigned."	"During your focus lesson, I observed how you used a think aloud to share examples and counterexamples. This is so useful for students especially when they are just learning a new math concept. This really helps them create mental pictures in their minds. How do you think your think aloud will change as you move to more abstract concepts?"

Source: Adapted from *Leading Student-Centered Coaching* (Sweeney & Mausbach, 2018).

Give Feedback: Feedback is required after *every* general walkthrough. If feedback isn't present, it is not a walkthrough; it is walking around. The key to feedback is to validate and teach. Using examples of teaching and learning taken from the classrooms provides concrete examples for teachers and helps them see that strategies can be successful in their context. We have found that it is important to provide whole staff, small group, and individual feedback. *Whole staff feedback* is typically included in the weekly message to staff and includes pictures of what was observed during the week that aligns with look fors. *Small group feedback* is provided during PLCs and will be discussed in Chapter 3. *Individual feedback* occurs after a general walkthrough via an email or sticky note left in the teacher's room. Using a combination of whole staff, small group (via PLCs), and individual methods ensures that feedback will be given.

> *Note This: Marshall (2013) is a strong advocate for face-to-face feedback, and we feel this is an effective method but not always doable in large schools, thus, leaders need to identify methods and techniques that work the best for them.*

The key is to make sure that feedback is given after *each* walkthrough and is qualitative, validating work that matches look fors, or noticing close approximations and promoting reflection. Figure 2.2 provides an example of feedback from a general walkthrough. The first row provides an example of feedback that describes and validates practices that match the look for. The second example in Figure 2.2 is used when practices observed don't exactly match the look for but are a close approximation. Again, the tone is positive and is designed to help teachers take the next steps in improving practice around the look for. The last row provides an example of reflective questions based on the look for that promotes thinking.

Assessment: Formative

Feedback Focus: Look Fors

This element's focus on building level change requires frequent doses of qualitative feedback to both individual teachers *and* the entire school. Feedback is narrative in form and is drawn from mutually defined look fors. As previously stated, the use of collaboratively developed look fors unify a school by helping create shared meaning and a common focus. Look fors establish standards for what the strategies in the school improvement plan will look and sound like when fully implemented. Without look fors, leaders can fall into the trap of thinking staff are resistant to change when the reality is they don't know or understand what they are being asked to implement. Look fors provide the clarity needed to help all staff achieve success and promote transparency which helps create a vibrant culture.

Look fors are an essential tool in the differentiated supervision model and are essential to the work in both Elements I and II. However, like any tool, if used improperly they are ineffective. Four key principles are fundamental

FIGURE 2.2 FEEDBACK EXAMPLE AFTER A GENERAL WALKTHROUGH

	EXAMPLE	WHAT THIS DOES	WHY IT MATTERS
Validate When observation shows *alignment* to looks fors	This week I was focusing on our look for "teachers use deep questions (Level 4 DOK) to determine student understanding." For example, one set of students was being asked to respond in writing to a series of important quotes from the novel they are reading. They had to describe the significance of the quote and what it implied about the character—very high-level activities. By using writing as a thinking strategy, this teacher can get a clear sense of EACH student's level of connection with the text without using lower level DOK questions.	Is specific and validates good practices	Raises level of awareness and promotes likelihood will occur again
Notice Close Approximation When observations show *close* approximation to look fors	This week I was focusing on our look for "teachers use deep questions (Level 4 DOK) to determine student understanding." I heard questions like, "Who was the protagonist?" "What is the theme?" These are building blocks for students. We need to remember that students need to know key ideas and details. Our ultimate goal is to get students to understand the author's meaning. Let's continue to focus on prompts that push kids to higher levels of thinking through our questioning by asking questions like, "What are significant quotes in the text that convey the author's purpose?" or "Choose three quotes that develop a theme."	Compliment and encourage by noticing close approximations	Pushes the goals of the school improvement and professional development (PD) plan
When observation shows *misalignment* to look fors Promote Reflection	This week I was focusing on our look for "teachers use deep questions (Level 4 DOK) to determine student understanding." This week I noticed a higher volume of open-ended questions being asked of students such as "How would you compare . . . ?" or "What do these two examples have in common?" Good examples of DOK 2 levels. How do these types of questions compare to the questions you are asking? How would you modify them to up the level of thinking for students?	Causes staff to reflect on areas of growth	Causes staff to reflect about their own practice, nudges teachers/school in the direction you want them to go

to ensuring that look fors provide support to teachers and leverage achievement (Mausbach & Morrison, 2016).

Look fors are as follows:

1. *Collaboratively developed by **all** staff.* The purpose of having a set of look fors is to help staff understand what the strategies in the plan will look like when they are in place. In a heightened sense of urgency to get them developed, a leader may be tempted to develop the list and hand out or worse use some developed by another school. It is both the process and the product that matter.

2. *Directly connected to the school improvement plan.* One of the primary purposes of look fors is to operationalize the school improvement plan. Thus, look fors must describe the strategies in the plan. Effective school improvement plans provide focus for a school and aligned look fors are essential for intense focus.

> *However, there will never be a perfect list of look fors. Develop a list and continue to provide professional learning support, but remember deep meaning will occur as staff implement–learning is the work (Fullan, 2009).*

3. *Connected to and build from teachers' current knowledge.* One of the biggest benefits of developing look fors is that the process deepens teachers' understanding of the initiative being implemented. This happens by engaging staff in learning around the initiative before developing the list. Without providing time for learning, the look fors may not be detailed or useful enough to provide feedback.

4. *Observable.* Look fors must be something that can be seen or heard and provide evidence of strategy implementation. They help a leader focus observations so meaningful feedback can be provided. Figure 2.3 illustrates the difference between look fors that promote clarity and those that do not.

FIGURE 2.3 DIFFERENCE BETWEEN WELL-CRAFTED AND POORLY CRAFTED LOOK FORS

WELL-CRAFTED LOOK FOR	POORLY CRAFTED LOOK FOR
Students know the purpose for learning and can articulate thinking strategies	Evidence of rigor and relevance
Teachers will ask questions, cues, and prompts during group work to inform next steps in instruction	Differentiate instruction
Teachers will model restorative language to acknowledge personal needs and interests (e.g., *I feel, I see you feeling, let's work together*, mentions of empathy dig opportunities)	Use restorative language

WHY IT WORKS

Facilitates Goal Setting

Picture those classrooms where teachers have clear and specific learning targets that guide their teaching. Students know what these are, and the entire classroom is working toward meeting these outcomes. The term well-oiled machine comes to mind when you spend time in these environments. Schools where teachers are clear about the building goals and benchmarks and the entire staff is working together through learning and collaboration also operate like a well-oiled machine. Just as learners struggle in classrooms that are chaotic, so do teachers in schools that lack clear and focused plans.

Goal setting as a leadership practice has an impact on student outcomes because it focuses and coordinates the work of adults around learning and achievement (Robinson, 2011). Clear goals help remove the noise found in many schools around competing agendas. It forces decisions about what is most important at the current moment in time. Being clear about the end game (goals) and how you are going to get there (strategies) is pivotal because it allows a leader to say no to competing initiatives and sets the stage for focused feedback. Armed with a skinny plan, a leader can focus efforts and help all staff work collectively toward mutually defined goals.

Improves Clarity

A coherent instructional program benefits both teachers and students. Students achieve at higher rates in schools with coherence (Fullan & Quinn, 2016; Newmann, Smith, Allensworth, & Bryk, 2001), and teachers develop stronger collaborative teams when they have a common approach to teaching and learning (Bryk, Sebring, Allensworth, Luppescu, & Easton, 2010). Achieving this coherence is not an easy task and requires a leader to pay particular attention to clarity in both communication and practice. Clarity necessitates a laser-like focus on creating a culture rich in inquiry, dialogue, and action around commonly defined practices. Common language is essential when defining practices, but doesn't always lead to common understanding (Dewitt, 2021). Understanding occurs when the practices are clearly defined *and* there is a continuous loop of dialogue around the impact from implementation attempts. Multiple opportunities to examine the impact of instructional practices, question their efficiency and effectiveness, and discuss implications are part of the learning journey. This can only happen when staff has clarity around what it is they are trying to do.

The differentiated supervision model promotes clarity by utilizing collaboratively defined look fors and providing ample doses of feedback that promote dialogue and reflection. The practices found in this element are designed to help ensure that all staff have ownership in where the school is headed and how they will get there. Connecting the school improvement and professional development plan to look fors and actionable feedback provides teachers with the necessary clarity and support needed to help students grow.

Builds Instructional Leadership

The last few decades have provided insight on the distinct ways principals can impact student learning. Robinson (2011) found "leading teacher learning and development" as having a 0.84 effect size on student achievement. A 0.40 effect size, the degree of impact a particular influence has on learning, reflects a year's progress, so 0.84 is significant. Focusing on learning experiences that improve teacher proficiency makes sense since the quality of the teacher has a direct impact on student achievement (Marzano, 2003). It is more productive, in terms of student growth, for a leader to devote their attention to planning, participating, and engaging in dialogue around teacher learning than spending inordinate amounts of time communicating and measuring performance standards, practices central to traditional modes of supervision. Timperley (2011) found that principals who focus on cultivating habits of mind were more successful than colleagues who spend time trying to meet individual teacher needs. Creating conditions for growth requires less weed pulling (focus on individual supervision) and more fertilizer (effective professional learning for all staff).

Moving an entire school forward requires the principal to act as a lead learner, focusing the building on a small number of specific goals for students while organizing learning that allows teachers to collectively learn from each other on how best to meet student needs. In doing this, the principal promotes what Fullan (2019) calls culture-based accountability, "individual and collective responsibility that becomes embedded into the values, behavior, and actions of people in the situation. . . . People in the culture embrace a focus on continuous improvement as something they have to do and prove to themselves and others" (p. 75). This requires the leader to "walk the talk" by collaborating with teachers to create a focused school improvement and PD plan and then work alongside staff as they learn and grow, signature practices in this element. The emphasis on focusing, organizing, clarifying, and participating in learning opportunities firmly places the principal in the role of lead learner, creating a culture of continuous improvement and growth.

MAKING IT HAPPEN

Infrastructure: Build Teams

So many times the term "buy-in" surfaces when talking about getting staff to engage in reform efforts. True engagement, however, requires a deeper level of commitment; it requires ownership. Leaders can't force this type of commitment, rather their influence lies in the environment they create (Senge, 2006). Staff are unable to own initiatives if they aren't a part of the process. This process requires principals to walk a fine line between getting bogged down taking an inordinate amount of time to develop the plan versus having staff simply "sign off" on the documents. Leaders navigate this by creating an infrastructure that allows all staff to systematically provide input and review progress on an ongoing basis.

The concept of a leadership team isn't new to schools; however, these teams typically address a variety of issues throughout the school. Tapping into a leadership team enables the principal to get relevant input from teachers. In this way, school improvement and professional learning are a priority and, in turn, create a guiding vision for staff.

Teachers should be able to select a goal area and work with that team. It is the principal's role to ensure that all staff members are represented on teams. For example, if a teacher is interested in math, she would serve on the team that is spearheading the work in this goal area. A member from each goal team would also serve on the overall school leadership team. This ensures that information developed and reviewed during team meetings can be shared throughout the school. The key is to have a structure and then to put the issues of school improvement as the focus of the agenda.

> *Note This: According to Mausbach and Morrison (2016), the number of leadership teams will vary depending on the size of the school, but as a rule of thumb, all instructional staff need to be engaged in school improvement planning.*

Develop a Layered Professional Development Plan

Joyce and Showers's (1980) seminal work on professional development (PD) structures that result in deep levels of implementation serves as the guidepost for organizing professional learning. As Figure 2.4 illustrates, the levels of support people need as they move from awareness to institutionalization of new practices must shift. Support needs to come in layers, meaning we have to give teachers opportunities to learn in large groups, small groups, and one-on-one simultaneously. Thus, we have to schedule and plan for these opportunities. The vehicle for doing this is the PD plan.

The PD plan includes two components: staff outcomes and the long-range plan.

Staff Outcomes

The outcomes section is simply identifying what staff will know and be able to do by the end of the school year. This list is generated from the strategies and action steps found in the school improvement plan. For example, if a strategy under the achievement goal is to utilize formative

FIGURE 2.4 PROFESSIONAL DEVELOPMENT STRUCTURES

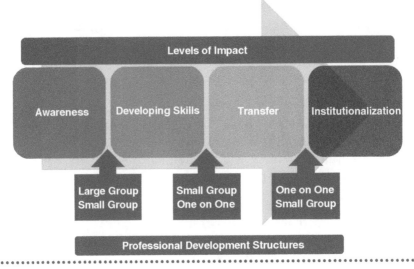

Source: Reprinted with permission from *School Leadership Through the Seasons* (Mausbach & Morrision, 2016).

assessments and one of the action steps is to implement questions, cues, and prompts, then one of the outcomes for staff would be that they could effectively use these questioning techniques to guide instruction. Developing a list of staff learning outcomes based on strategies and action steps helps to identify if the school improvement plan makes sense and is achievable. Professional development will feel fragmented and meaningless, like the flavor of the month, if it isn't derived from the school improvement plan. Figure 2.5 provides an example of this section of the PD plan. Creating a list of outcomes makes the work ahead clearly visible and helps to determine if the plan needs to be pared down.

FIGURE 2.5 PROFESSIONAL DEVELOPMENT PLAN EXAMPLE: STAFF OUTCOMES

By the end of the year, our staff will be able to know/do the following:

OUTCOMES	GOAL/STRATEGY
Write quality learning targets to guide daily lessons both in academics and mindfulness (good work habits)	Goal 1-Strategy 1 Goal 2-Strategy 2
Implement effective mini lessons	Goal 1-Strategy 1
Embed checks for understanding strategies into instructional practice (mini lessons)	Goal 1-Strategy 1
Utilize a problem-solving model around restorative practice	Goal 2-Strategy 2

Long-Range Plan

A detailed long-range plan comprises the second and most lengthy component of the PD plan. The PD plan is fluid, and as principals gather evidence of strategy implementation, observe in classrooms, and analyze student work, adjustments will be made. However, without a tentative long-range (1 year) plan for professional growth, the learning of teachers can fall prey to the dreaded "activity" trap, treating PD as a series of events that are loosely coupled, lack relevance, and have little hope of impacting teaching and learning. This section of the plan identifies topics for large and small group learning *every* week of the school year. Having this in hand at the beginning of the school year helps the leader not waste any valuable time and also serves as a connector for one-on-one learning that may occur through coaching cycles and principal feedback. See Appendix B for an example of a school improvement and PD plan.

Utilize Look Fors

Look fors are an effective tool in the differentiated supervision model, but only when utilized. Like the handy Swiss Army knife, look fors are multifunctional, providing leaders with two important mechanisms: a process for leveraging effective feedback and a method of assessing staff learning. Becoming skilled in using this tool is central to the work of the school leader in this model.

Use look fors to leverage feedback. Look fors are an effective supervision tool because they help the leader provide bite-sized chunks of meaningful feedback to teachers. Unlike complicated checklists and rubrics that entail every aspect of teaching imaginable, look fors distill a teaching strategy into clear and complete statements that describe what will be seen or heard when implemented. This provides a descriptive target and allows the leader to focus on one piece of feedback at a time.

> *Giving less feedback, more often, maximizes teacher development (Brambrick-Santoyo, 2012).*

Look fors that lead to rich qualitative feedback require leaders to pay attention to how they are developed. The key to the development process is to make sure that all staff have the opportunity to contribute to and collaborate on the looks fors. Development of an initial look for list doesn't have to be a time-consuming process, and perfection isn't the goal. The goal is clarity and shared understanding. Utilizing the guiding questions found in Figure 2.6 is helpful in ensuring look fors are descriptive enough to be useful. Appendix C provides an example of a protocol for developing look fors with staff.

FIGURE 2.6 GUIDING QUESTIONS WHEN DEVELOPING LOOK FORS

Is the look for more than one or two words?

Is the look for a complete thought or sentence?

Is the look for something you could *see or hear* if you walked into a classroom?

Is the look for written in plain language that a non-educator could understand?

Once the collaboratively developed look fors are in place, the principal uses them to provide feedback after the general walkthrough. The general walkthrough is the vehicle to determine if the school improvement plan is being implemented, at what levels, and to identify what support staff need next in order to get to deeper levels of implementation. Using collaboratively developed look fors around strategies identified in the school improvement plan ensures that the general walkthrough isn't an inspection or "gotcha." The staff knows what the principal is looking for and knows that feedback will validate the teaching and learning practices found in the look fors. The purpose of feedback is to lift all staff. This doesn't happen by pointing out deficits, rather growth occurs when practices that are aligned with look fors are validated. Figure 2.3 provided examples of this type of feedback, aligned to look fors.

Treat the look for process as a formative measure of staff learning. Utilizing feedback to monitor student learning and adjust instruction has been well established as an effective practice that deepens learning (0.66 effect size according to Hattie, 2019). Creating these same conditions when organizing adult learning can be challenging and is why using collaboratively developed looks fors is such a critical practice. Spending time discussing, identifying, and articulating what a strategy looks like in practice surfaces the collective understanding of staff. The dialogue necessary to create look fors helps the leader discern what aspects of the initiative are understood and where there may be misconceptions. Determining the shared understanding of the staff allows the leader to make adjustments to professional learning. In other words, it provides the leader with a method to formatively assess staff and then respond in a way that helps them continue to learn and grow.

Consider the following example from a school that was trying to implement restorative practices. The left-hand column in Figure 2.7 outlines the set of look fors developed in September after the staff had engaged in learning in the summer and fall. Upon reflection on the conversations during the development process and the resulting look fors, the leader realized that staff's understanding was superficial and without a deeper dive they would never be able to adjust their practice. Armed with this understanding, the leader decided that staff would need more tangible strategies in order to use restorative practices and see the benefits. Thus, the leader decided to dig into Ross Greene's (2014) problem-solving model with a focus on using empathy digs. After several months of learning and using empathy digs, staff came back together and developed the revised version found in the right-hand column of Figure 2.7. This version not only showed evidence of how much the staff had deepened their understanding, but also provided the leader with direction for staff learning in the upcoming year.

FIGURE 2.7 RESTORATIVE PRACTICES LOOK FORS

	INITIAL VERSION: FALL	REVISED VERSION: SPRING
Teacher	• Teachers show respect by using the appropriate tone of voice. • Teachers identify behaviors that disrupt the educational process in a calm way, and use modeling to encourage positive behavior. • Teachers engage with students in a manner that acknowledges their personal needs and interests. • Teachers model active listening skills.	• Teachers will use restorative language when working with students to solve problems (*I feel, I see you feeling, Let's work together*, etc.). • Teachers will start the problem-solving process with students by gathering information from the students' perspective about the problem they are working to solve (empathy dig). • Teachers will use students' interests and needs to promote positive relationships.
Student	• Students express their thoughts and feelings using school-appropriate language. • Students reflect (verbally or in writing) on how their choices impact others. • Students actively engage in the learning process by participating in instruction and independently beginning tasks. • Students practice preventative strategies for avoiding/managing conflict.	• Students express their thoughts and feelings using school-appropriate language. • Students will be able to explain, either verbally or in writing, how their choices help or harm themselves and others. • Students will be able to reference and utilize tools (peace corners, anchor charts, visual cues, mindfulness breaks) within the classroom.
Environment	• Room arrangements allow for collaboration. • Space is dedicated to allow for restorative conversations (safe space).	• Morning circles will be used to build social-emotional skills. • Anchor charts that promote social and emotional problem-solving strategies will be displayed. • Space dedicated for restorative conversations.

Organize Feedback

One of the benefits of the differentiated supervision model for leaders is that they develop a rich sense of teachers' practices due to the frequency of observations. A benefit for teachers is that they receive feedback after every observation. Over the course of a year, this generates a treasure trove of information. However, this knowledge is useful only when it can be easily retrieved. Capturing what was observed and the subsequent feedback given provides valuable insights into patterns and trends in teachers' growth. A system for easily accessing this data is required. We advocate for simple solutions we call the feedback journal and walk-through summary.

Feedback Journal

The feedback journal is a spreadsheet that tracks observations and feedback by teachers. Each teacher has a tab in the spreadsheet. Basic information is included on this form: dates and times the teacher was observed, a brief description of what was observed, and a summary of the feedback (rein-forcement, refinement, reflective questions). Each observation is captured on a separate line on the teacher's sheet. Figure 2.8 provides an example of a feedback log. Notice the teacher names on the bottom tabs; the example shows Mrs. N's data.

The feedback journal is a tool for the principal. It is a place to capture observations and corresponding feedback so leaders can discern what is improving over time and what isn't. It is difficult to determine appropriate levels of support without this big picture look. This tool helps leaders determine next steps based on ongoing evidence from the teacher's practice. Capturing this valuable information in a straightforward manner promotes reflection and helps the leader identify how best to meet the teacher's individual needs.

Walkthrough Summary

In addition to the feedback log, we have found another important tool in organizing and utilizing information from observations, the walkthrough summary. The walkthrough summary provides a "birds-eye view" of the entire school, providing valuable information about the current reality of the building. Figure 2.9 provides an example of the walkthrough summary tool. This form includes who was observed and the focus of the walkthrough based on look fors. Each week the teachers are observed and are categorized as strong, approaching, and need support.

This provides two very valuable pieces of information. First, it identifies if there is a teacher in need of more assistance. Instead of waiting for the teacher to continue to struggle, leaders can begin to provide support imme-diately. Second, it helps the leader gauge how much more professional

FIGURE 2.8 FEEDBACK JOURNAL EXAMPLE

Date of Observation	Time	Content Area	Brief Description of What was Observed	Feedback to Reinforce	Feedback to Refine	Reflective Question	Other Notes
9/17/2021	10:00	number talk	Students were around the white board in the back of the room. The problem was number patterns. Students stated their strategy in the solving the number problem. Mrs. Nagel wrote student name and strategy on the	Students feel comfortable with solving and sharing their thinking around the problem. You captured their learning well.	Using a lot of funnel questions, need to think about how to ask more focused questions	Do you think your questioning leads students to a certain strategy?	Mrs. N and I discussed what her purpose of h talk was. She said she was trying to get stude recognize math facts. So we discussed quest the difference in questions leading to a certair
9/28/2021	10:10	number talk	Student were really ready to answer, they were giving the thumb signal and wanted to share out. Great astrmophere for students so willing to share out.	Great leaning environment,	Planning the problems so they help students use a varity of strategies for solvi g	Where do you get your problems? Are you doing a Problem Solving String or random problems?	We talked about where she is getting the num from. Going back to the book and do the strinç strategy. Capturing the learning on an Anchor students may reference.
			students were in various groups around the room working on various tasks. Each group had something	Students were in various groups - working in partners or individually on		I noticed you were working with what I would call the upper group and your para had more of the lower	Mr. N and I discussed how in our PLC we we discussing how to push our top students even when discussing learning progressions - not tu think of scaffolding the lesson for the middle le how to take tasks and make them more challe more work for those students but more rigorou

Mr. T ▾   Ms. F. ▾   Mrs. N. ▾   Ms. S ▾   Mr. C ▾   Ms. C ▾   Mrs. L ▾   Mrs. K ▾   Ms. H ▾   Hrbek ◂ ▸

FIGURE 2.9 WALKTHROUGH SUMMARY TOOL

KEY							
Strong/At Standard							
Approaching							
Need Support							
WEEK	**AUG. 7**	**SEPT. 3**	**SEPT. 13**	**SEPT. 20**	**SEPT. 27**	**OCT. 4**	**OCT. 11**
Observation Focus	Clear Learning Targets & Success Criteria				Think Aloud/Modeling		
Teachers Observed at Green	Naughton, Jones, Smith, King, Peterson	Long, McGee, McPherson, Harvey, Donohue, Flanagan	Homer, Lemon, Fey, Grafton, Cash, Griffin				
Teachers Observed at Yellow	Miller, Anderson, J. Smith	Crouch, Frazier, Howells	Humble, Lowe				
Teachers Observed at Red	Piedmont		Grass				

learning is needed in a particular area and who needs it the most. This allows the principal to pinpoint small group learning as well as utilize those teachers at green to help model and support their peers.

EQUITY CHECK

"When staff is clear on what quality looks like for all, they can more easily make adjustments when learning isn't as predicted."

An equitable school is one where each student gets what they need to succeed. Creating this requires recognizing the nuanced relationship between equal and equitable. As Smith, Frey, Pumpian, and Fisher (2017) adeptly describe it, "In an equal school situation, we build staircases that learners can ascend to higher levels of achievement; in an equitable one, we make sure to build ramps alongside those staircases" (p. 2). The staircases and ramps work best when there is clarity on the destination. Agreeing on the fundamental learning experiences for all students creates shared understanding making it easier to construct scaffolds when needed. Clear school goals and strategies coupled with collaboratively developed look fors lay a foundation of equity. When staff is clear on what quality looks like for all, they can more easily make adjustments when learning isn't as predicted. The practices in this element make certain that school improvement and supervision processes are aligned in support of teacher and student learning.

FROM THE FIELD

At Issue: Gail worked with her leadership team and staff to develop a focused school improvement and PD plan. She realized that to meet the goals set she needed to monitor the plan and attend to the needs of all classrooms. It was time to focus on the work.

Gail's team identified ambitious goals to raise proficiency in reading and math by 15% and meet expected growth targets. The strategy in the school improvement plan was to implement learning targets and success criteria within a framework of Gradual Release of Responsibility (Pearson & Gallagher, 1983). A focused PD plan was developed that included a series of learning opportunities designed to increase staff's knowledge and use of learning targets and success criteria. Staff engaged in weekly professional learning for the first month of school to develop initial shared meaning on learning targets and success criteria. Once staff had foundational knowledge, Gail engaged the entire staff in developing look fors.

Gail had a staff of 80 teachers, so she developed a plan to monitor progress by conducting general walkthroughs using feedback cycles that allowed her to get into every classroom at least once every 3 weeks. Using her staff blog, Gail provided weekly feedback sharing examples of implementation based on look fors. There were weeks that she shared strong examples and others where she noticed only close approximations. Every blog included an opportunity for teachers to reflect on their practice. She used this opportunity to provide building-wide feedback to her staff that validated practice and provided a specific model for what it could look and sound like in teachers' classrooms. Gail was consistent; she went through the feedback loops and stayed diligent in sharing building feedback. Because the goals were ambitious, Gail made sure to take a tone that encouraged staff. As the year progressed, teachers began to reflect on their practice and develop confidence utilizing the school improvement strategies and action steps. Staff were heard to say things like, "I have really grown this year as an educator. I think that is due to all the feedback and focused learning we have done," and "The high expectations and clear feedback have made an impact on my classroom practice."

When assessments were given, the achievement needle moved, and eventually, as predicted, the goals were inching closer to becoming a reality. Teachers found that success was the best stress relief and celebrated their accomplishments together.

"A rising tide lifts all boats," a quote made popular by John F. Kennedy, is the mantra of this element. Raising student achievement in a school requires attention to all the boats in the harbor. To implement this, be sure of the following:

- The general walkthrough and qualitative feedback provide direction so all teachers can work together toward a common goal.

- There is a layered PD plan aligned to the school improvement focus.

- Collaboratively defined look fors provide clarity so teachers know exactly what strategies "looks like and sounds like" when implemented.

- Ongoing feedback is provided weekly to ensure that all teachers see strong models to improve practice.

A garden flourishes when the gardener has a bird's-eye view of all the plants and is able to monitor growth. High quality PD and look fors sprinkled in with regular doses of qualitative feedback till the soil for improvement. Tending to the entire system ensures that sustainable growth becomes a reality.

WHERE ARE YOU NOW?

Creating a culture of growth happens when a leader's mindset is focused on helping others develop their talents. Specific knowledge and skills are needed for this to come to fruition. Rate yourself on the statements below and identify ways you can move along the continuum.

Getting started — Practices firmly in place

Planting seeds

Blooming

Knowledge	I understand the professional development staff needs in order to enact strategies in the school improvement plan. This is evidenced by a list of professional learning staff outcomes for the year and a detailed plan for achieving them.
	I understand the benefits of large group, small group, and individual learning and have organized professional learning to provide opportunities for all three.
Skills	Look fors were developed in collaboration with all staff and are used to provide feedback to staff.
	I connect the school improvement plan to the work in the other elements.
	Feedback includes a rationale (the why) for the practices that were validated.
Follow Through	I share weekly feedback with staff that validates the look fors observed during general walkthroughs. Feedback describes what was observed and why it is important in helping students succeed.
	I have a method for documenting feedback so I can frequently review to look for patterns and trends across the school.

CHAPTER 3

....

ELEMENT II
Individual/Small Group Support With Qualitative Feedback

"The practices in this element act as the compost for change because they accelerate growth and ensure a vibrancy in the implementation of new learning."

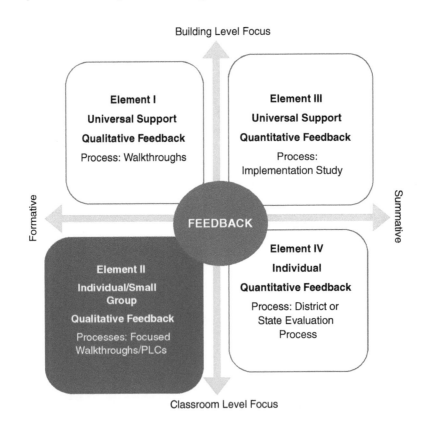

Building Level Focus

Element I
Universal Support
Qualitative Feedback
Process: Walkthroughs

Element III
Universal Support
Quantitative Feedback
Process:
Implementation Study

Formative

FEEDBACK

Summative

Element II
Individual/Small Group
Qualitative Feedback
Processes: Focused
Walkthroughs/PLCs

Element IV
Individual
Quantitative Feedback
Process: District or
State Evaluation
Process

Classroom Level Focus

What Keeps Us Up at Night: Have you ever worried that some kids were getting better instruction than others in your school? Results across teachers, grades levels, and teams seem to have a high degree of variance even when you have provided teachers with the same opportunities to learn and grow. How can you balance the needs of individuals, grade levels, and teams in an efficient, manageable, impactful way so all kids get what they need?

The purpose of schooling is student learning. While this makes sense in theory, in practice the day-to-day reality of schools can find leaders engaging in a myriad of things that detract from this mission. Helping leaders keep the focus on learning is the driver for the differentiated supervision model and nowhere is this more apparent than in the 21work employed in Element II. Practices in this element connect both student learning and teaching. Narrowing the focus on learning happens when teaching practices and student outcomes are intermingled in a manner that informs teachers about what's working and why and vice versa. Gardens thrive when plant growth is monitored, but also when careful consideration is given to the conditions that contribute to this growth. This same notion holds true for kids and teachers.

The practices in this element act as the compost for change because they accelerate growth and ensure a vibrancy in the implementation of new learning. This is accomplished through heavy doses of qualitative feedback provided to both individual teachers and small groups (i.e., PLCs). The continuous cycle of observation found in this element ensures that feedback is relevant to day-to-day instruction, upping the likelihood that it will be utilized to inform and change practice.

> *The majority of a principal's time is spent in this element because of the direct impact seen in classrooms.*

CLARIFYING THE MODEL

Focus: Classroom

Examining classroom instruction, so rich feedback can be provided and acted upon, is the focus of the practices found in this element. Two primary processes are used to make this happen: 1) active participation in PLCs and 2) conducting focused walkthroughs.

PLC Participation

The PLC is the primary mechanism for teacher learning. Fisher, Frey, Almarode, Flories, and Nagel (2020) said it best, "If we want to change the learning in our school or classroom, we have to change our teaching. If we want to change our teaching, we have to change our decisions and our thinking" (p. 13). Working together is one of the most powerful mechanisms for helping teachers change their thinking and practices. The impact of effective collaboration is why the PLC process has been widely accepted as a method for facilitating student growth (Dufour, 2007). However, as Fisher et al. (2020) point out, the singular focus on student learning may hinder the impact of PLCs. Exploring both learning *and* teaching issues as part of collaborative work is necessary if we desire rigorous learning experiences for all students. PLCs are the place where teachers wrestle with the thorny issues of teaching *and* learning. Therefore, it is only logical then that they play a central role in the supervision process.

Active participation in PLCs requires leaders to attend meetings once a week. While this may seem daunting, can you imagine a coach who doesn't attend practice or team meetings? That notion is absurd—too much important business takes place during those sessions, and coaches need that context to be an effective leader. The same is true for PLCs because this is where the SIP plan gets enacted. PLCs are where teachers work together to apply teaching strategies, assess impact relative to predetermined success criteria, and seek to understand what worked and what didn't so adjustments to classroom practice can be made. These topics are too important for leaders to miss out on, so they must be active participants during teachers' collaboration. Making the time to participate once a week, no matter the size of the school, can happen but requires foresight and planning on the part of the principal. Strategies discussed in Chapter 2 around creating the infrastructure for support are critical. Upfront planning and clarity around who and when leaders will meet with each team is essential.

Participate Rather Than Dominate

Note that we aren't advocating for principals to take over these meetings—what we are advocating for is the principal (and assistant principals) to be active members of the team. Their role is to support teachers as they work to improve their practice, while learning alongside them about what is making a difference for students. The degree of principal leadership depends on the team's efficiency and results. Within all schools, the functioning of teams varies. Their growth won't be identical nor will their results. Teams that work well together and have good results with their students will need less support than teams that have difficulty working together and achieve lower results. The leader's role will be differentiated based on the team's needs. The bottom line is that leaders need to be actively engaged during team collaboration. This involvement isn't about micromanaging; rather it is about the leader developing the group by creating a collective culture of efficacy (Fullan, 2014).

Focused Walkthrough

The focused walkthrough, unlike the general walkthrough described in Chapter 2, is designed to target observations of teaching and learning for a longer period of time (10–20 minutes) in a classroom or series of classrooms. The focused walkthrough is used when the leader wants to follow up or learn more around a teaching and learning issue that is related to school improvement strategies or a potential issue that has surfaced through the general walkthrough or PLC meetings.

Like Marshall's (2013) mini observations, the focused walkthrough allows the leader to home in on specific instructional issues in order to help either a) diagnose why results aren't happening for students or b) reinforce/refine teachers' implementation of a strategy. The issues teachers are wrestling with, either individually or in their PLC, and how they plan to solve them serve as focal points in a focused walkthrough. For example, a team might be trying to help second-grade students understand rounding whole numbers. After analyzing student work, the team notices that students are confused about place value. The team decides to do a mini lesson on place value and determine learning intentions and success criteria. They discuss what it will look like and sound like when students are successful. Armed with information, the principal makes sure to spend more time in the second-grade classrooms during math the next week, providing feedback around the success criteria identified during the PLC.

> *Teachers should be aware of the purpose of focused walkthroughs because they are directly tied to PLC meetings and one-on-one discussions.*

Like general walkthroughs, the key is to make sure that teachers have a clear understanding of the focus of the observations. Feedback is a critical component and typically face-to-face feedback is both the easiest and the most powerful. In fact, since teachers have been working on the issue with the leader, they are often anxious to have a discussion around what was observed.

Assessment: Formative

Feedback Focus: Reinforcement, Refinement, and Reflection

This element's focus on classroom level change requires frequent doses of qualitative feedback to small groups and individual teachers. Similar to Element I, feedback is narrative in form and is drawn from mutually defined look fors. It is brief and typically includes three components: reinforcement, refinement, and reflection. Figure 3.1 describes each of these three components and provides examples.

Like the children in our schools, teams don't all start at the same level nor do they develop at the same rate. The differentiated supervision model takes

FIGURE 3.1 THREE RS OF FEEDBACK

Reinforcement	Reinforcing feedback identifies and *validates* observed practices that were aligned to look fors. The purpose is to help promote the likelihood that the teacher will engage in this practice again because they understand what worked and why that matters.
	Example: Your pace during the focus lesson was quick and efficient. You attended to specific students when they were in guided practice. Because you listened to student feedback, you realized that you needed to be clearer in your questioning.
Refinement	Refining feedback identifies an area where observed practices were observed that do not align with the look fors or were not effective as utilized. The purpose is to help the teacher or team think about what actions need to be taken in order to improve practice.
	Example: We have been talking about how important conversation moves are during the focus lesson. Moves such as "add on," "paraphrase," and "restate" are efficient strategies to use during math instruction. Consider planning and utilizing time within your PLC to implement these moves.
Reflection	Reflection feedback involves posing a question based on the reinforcement and/or refinement feedback. The purpose is to help the teacher think more deeply about instructional practice.
	Example: How do the questions you ask during focused instruction help you gauge student understanding?

this into account by providing feedback based on need rather than a generic checklist. Effective leaders scrutinize team dynamics and the context of the work to identify the level of functioning and adjust support accordingly. The frequency of observations doesn't change when working in this element. At a minimum, teachers should be observed every 3 weeks as outlined in Chapter 1. What shifts in this element is purpose. Element I is focused more specifically on the school improvement plan, while the purpose here is to provide additional support to the individual teacher or team based on areas of need identified through general and focused walkthroughs and weekly PLC meetings. The quality of feedback suffers greatly if leaders can't connect the learning happening in the PLC to practices in the classroom. Leveraging the important learning that takes place in the PLC requires the principal to follow up via observation and feedback.

Student Evidence

One of the most critical components of this element is the use of student evidence during PLCs. The real work students do day-to-day serves as the vehicle for determining actions and leads to feedback that will have the greatest impact. Interim assessments and benchmark data play an important role in the assessment puzzle, but are not nearly as important as the use of student evidence. This type of data has elevated status because it provides ongoing information in real time.

Student evidence is the best formative data available to teachers and leaders, and without this information, collaborative work falls flat.

Leveraging student evidence requires teams to engage in inquiry around learning targets and success criteria. This is critical because it helps the team develop a rich understanding of what students need to learn and, equally important, how they will know learning has happened. Armed with this clarity, the principal can support the team and individual teachers in the pursuit of this learning. Making this happen requires a focus on protocols that analyze student evidence in order to determine what impact teacher actions have had on the learner. We advocate for the use of protocols that focus on using evidence, provide ample time for analysis, and end with action. The team and the principal are then armed with a straightforward plan of action providing the focus and clarity needed to improve practice.

> *Student evidence includes writing samples, reading responses, exit slips, open-ended math problems, anecdotal notes, and problem-solving tasks—any work that makes learning visible.*

WHY IT WORKS

Creates a Structure for Interdependence

The good news is we know what works when it comes to professional learning. High quality professional development involves collaboration, is conducted in context, and it allows for experimentation and feedback (Darling-Hammond, 1998; Fullan, Hill, & Crevlola, 2006; Hattie, 2009). Collaboration is a powerful way to change teaching practice when it involves joint work, which includes critical inquiry, sustained scrutiny of practice, analysis, and debate in search of improvement (Little, 1990). Joint work, according to Little, goes beyond storytelling; aiding and assisting; or sharing ideas, methods, and opinions. Joint work is characterized by teachers' collective action and a level of interdependence where individual success is contingent upon the work of the group. This sophisticated level of interdependence requires leaders to understand the complexity of the system they are working in and then thoughtfully and deliberately organize learning so that connections can be formed (Donohoo & Mausbach, 2021).

Schools are complex systems, which means they are made up of interconnected parts. The interdependence inherent in a system results in a ripple effect: One thing is touched and other parts of the system are affected. A gardener avoids counterproductive practices like putting plants that need shade in spots where they get full sun. They figure out how to have the parts of the soil, seeds, and weather conditions work in concert rather than in competition. The differentiated supervision model works because it develops positive interdependence through connecting building, team, and individual learning so they work together in service of student growth. The practices in Element II promote positive interdependence through the tasks teachers engage in when working together. Teachers' work becomes naturally interconnected when they labor to figure out how to assess student learning, analyze student evidence around learning targets, and plan next steps in instruction. Learning alongside teachers during PLCs and providing feedback and support, the hallmarks of the leader's work in this element, encourage the level of interdependence necessary for quality joint work.

Collective Teacher Efficacy Requires Collaboration

The belief that together we can make a difference on outcomes for students is the essence of collective teacher efficacy (Goddard, Hoy, & Woolfolk Hoy, 2004). Learning flourishes in an environment where both adults and students believe they have what it takes to be successful. This is why collective teacher efficacy is such a powerful influence on student achievement, with a 1.39 effect size. Considering that a 0.40 effect size equals a year's worth of growth, collective efficacy has the potential to quadruple the rate of student learning (Donohoo, 2017; Hattie, 2015).

Given the potential impact of collective teacher efficacy, leaders must possess a sense of urgency about creating the conditions that increase the likelihood that it will permeate throughout the school. Donohoo (2017) has identified six enabling conditions: advanced teacher influence, goal consensus, teacher's knowledge about one another's work, cohesive staff, responsiveness of leadership, and effective systems of intervention. Each of these conditions shows up in the work of Element II. When teachers work in teams setting goals, adjusting curriculum and instruction, analyzing each other's student work, and monitoring effectiveness of interventions, they become empowered to own the work of school improvement. Teachers see firsthand the impact their decisions have on the instructional climate of the school, which in turn increases efficacy and ownership (Ross, Hogaboam-Gray, & Gray, 2004).

Collective efficacy can flow out of this work, but not without a tuned-in leader. Leaders must have a pulse on what is occurring in classrooms and during PLCs so they can respond accordingly. When teachers experience success, engage with effective models, are provided feedback, and feel safe to take risks, their efficacy grows (Bandura, 1997). This requires working arm in arm with teachers to establish goals and expectations, to interpret results and provide feedback, and to ensure that teacher voice and leadership have an opportunity to flourish (Donohoo, 2017). The leadership practices in Element II directly align with this research, resulting in increased collective teacher efficacy. Making time for these practices is not optional since the stakes are too high for our students for leaders to ignore.

High Impact Teams Don't Just Happen

Far too often leaders make assumptions that staff know how to work together and that this work is productive. According to Fullan and Quinn (2016), "Collaboration as an end in itself is a waste of time. Groups are powerful, which means that they can be powerfully wrong. Getting together without the discipline and specificity of collective deliberation can be a grand waste of time" (p.13). Leaders can be lulled into thinking that teams are functioning because they meet regularly, have team norms, and use agendas. Elisa MacDonald (2013) calls this the instant coffee approach to leading teams because the learning results in the same richness as an instant cup of coffee—not much. The goal for a leader is to have high functioning, high-impact teams. This means that the teams not only work well together, but their work results in improved outcomes for students (MacDonald, 2013). Achieving this level of teaming requires a leader to intentionally coordinate collaborative work so it has a direct impact on student outcomes.

One of the characteristics of productive teams is stable settings (Gallimore, Emerling, Saunders, & Goldenberg, 2009). Stable settings refer to protected time and the principal's commitment to the process. Growing and developing teams require leaders who can help teams navigate the hurdles that are inherent when working together to solve complex problems. They need to make sure that teams have the tools they need to be productive. Without an ongoing presence at team meetings, a leader has a difficult time knowing the level of team functioning which results in a lack of understanding about the frequency and type of support needed to improve student results.

The work in collaborative teams directly influences individual development. Considering who is on the team, how well they are working together, and what they are working on expedites a leader's ability to support individual teachers. Instructional concerns can surface immediately through the ongoing process of analyzing student work, cueing the principal to spend more time or take a deeper look in a classroom where performance is lagging. The ability to address issues in real time circumvents minor issues from becoming major problems. Providing the right scaffolds at the right time is as essential for teachers as it is for students. This model, and the practices found in this element, make this happen when leaders tend to team function and impact.

MAKING IT HAPPEN

The work in this element hinges on effective collaborative teaming. The strategic development of the team reaps double dividends because of the influence this work has on both group and individual growth. Helping teams function at high levels requires the use of intentional practices by the leader so that this work delivers on the promise of improved outcomes for students.

Infrastructure: Build Meaningful Collaboration

Three important footings must be in place in order to have meaningful collaboration take place: 1) making time to meet, 2) having clear outcomes for each meeting, and 3) using student evidence to make decisions.

Making Time: The obvious first step in building infrastructure is creating time for teams to meet. While this seems straightforward, leaders have to be cognizant of frequency and time of day. There is no definitive answer in terms of frequency. However, there is some research to suggest that when teachers collaborate three or more times per week collective efficacy perceptions are significantly and positively affected (Johnson, 2012). Thus, minimum expectations would be once a week—once or twice a month will not suffice. When teachers meet with this level of frequency, they are provided the time and space to design, deliver, and debrief lessons. They can draw on each other's experiences and expertise, pooling ideas, methods, and materials, the type of work that increases collective efficacy. Without this continuous engagement, teams will have difficulty moving past the "divide and conquer" mentality that has teams splitting up duties in order to complete tasks.

Identifying Clear Outcomes & a Structure: PLCs must have a purpose and a stated outcome for every meeting. A clearly defined purpose helps keep the group focused and helps to ensure that time spent in learning teams results in changes in classroom practices and, more importantly, student outcomes. It isn't until teachers see how this time directly relates to the teaching and learning issues faced in their classroom that they will see the value of this work. This won't happen without a clear outcome and accompanying plan for the learning time. Starting every meeting by collaboratively developing the outcome and ending with a summary and focus for the next meeting time is a critical feature of high-impact, high-functioning teams. The principal needs to help support these outcomes by providing learning resources during team time, asking probing questions that help the team think richly about the issue, and summarizing and clarifying when there are misconceptions.

Having a common structure for PLC time helps utilize the time most efficiently and helps create a rhythm to the work. It also aids in having the team determine what they want to accomplish during their time together. The format found in Figure 3.2 is used to help ensure that the meeting flows and outcomes are realized. The meeting starts with revisiting norms and a warm-up activity around mission that helps connect previous work and purpose. Next, the team defines the outcome for the meeting. The analysis and decision-making portion of the meeting includes reviewing data and

FIGURE 3.2 STRUCTURE FOR LEARNING TEAMS

PHASE	QUESTION	PURPOSE
Warm-Up	What is our fundamental purpose, what do we value, and how do we know?	Remind staff of previous work and connect to the mission (purpose) of the school. Develop ownership in the work.
Collaboratively Develop Outcome	What is our learning intention for today?	Keeps the discussion on track and ensures the team meets objectives.
Analysis and Decision-Making	*Questions used during this phase will be determined by learning intention. Following are example questions:* What is student work telling us about student learning? What do students know? What do we want students to be able to do? What strategies did you use to achieve positive achievement in your classroom? What should we do next? What strategies could we use that would help students grow?	Determine action based on data.
Reflection	What have you accomplished during this PLC to respond to student achievement? What actions are you taking as a result of our discussion today?	Increase collective teacher efficacy.

resources around the guiding question for the meeting. Once the question is answered, teachers plan how to respond to the data in practical terms in their classrooms. This predictable routine helps to ensure that the work is focused on students and isn't dependent on the principal leading the group.

Using Student Evidence: The key to using student evidence is not just collecting, but using it to help inform instruction. The principal needs to make sure that formative data being collected on students is used to answer the question, "Is learning taking place?" Standard processes for data collection and retrieval need to be in place so PLC time can be spent identifying practices that are in response to the data. This data may be as formal as district common assessments or as simple as a checklist developed for a unit of study by the team. It's not so much about the assessment as it is about the use of the assessment. Does the team know if core instruction and interventions are working? If not, what needs to happen next? Many times, this results in the need for a focused walkthrough in order to help answer this question. The data from focused walkthroughs helps the team pinpoint effective practices. Data is the fuel for effective PLC work, and it's the conversation that moves learning forward.

Connect Building Professional Development to Team Learning

A basic tenant of this model is providing teachers with what they need based on their current level of understanding. One of the ways this gets actualized is through differentiated support to teams. A recursive action planning process provides a vehicle for making this happen. The purpose of this method is to provide teams with a mechanism that allows them to identify and direct their learning in a manner that contributes to achieving overall building goals. The work identified through this process provides content for the previously shared structure identified in the previous section. Figure 3.3 outlines the steps in the process.

The process begins with having the team develop shared meaning by unpacking the look fors developed by the entire staff. Allowing teams the opportunity to take a deeper dive into clarifying what look fors mean in practice strengthens the teams' function by providing a solid foundation of understanding that can be accessed when problem-solving on student learning issues. The process focuses teachers' attention on their levels of implementation and how they have or have not impacted student results. Figure 3.4 is an example of one team's unpacked look fors around teacher clarity.

FIGURE 3.3 RECURSIVE TEAM ACTION PLANNING PROCESS

FIGURE 3.4 UNPACKING LOOK FORS ORGANIZER

LOOK FOR	WHY IS IT IMPORTANT	TEACHER BEHAVIOR (LOOKS LIKE, SOUNDS LIKE)	STUDENT BEHAVIOR (LOOKS LIKE, SOUNDS LIKE)	ENVIRONMENTAL EVIDENCE
Learning intentions and success criteria are written for a standard, and not specific to certain lessons or tasks.	Students are able to explain how the task is aligned to the LI/standard. Understanding the standard is important to develop progressions of learning. Sets expectations for achieving grade-level standards.	Referring to LI/SC before, during, and after the lesson. Using academic vocabulary throughout the lesson. Using talk moves (repeating, revoicing, turn & talk, wait time, reasoning). Teacher questioning to scaffold student learning—students are leading the learning. Instruction and pacing are concise and focused.	Can restate/explain what they have learned or what they are expected to learn. Using language of LI/SC/ academic vocabulary 80% of students or more would be proficient. Students engaged in discourse. Students are engaged and taking ownership and initiative of their learning.	LI/SC posted in the room. Student work aligned to LI/SC. Anchor charts reflect the important learning. Language of LI/SC matches the standard. Rigorous student work that matches the standard. Teachers examining student work.
Teacher references learning intentions and success criteria before, during, and after the lesson.	Establishes focus and clarity. As the lesson progresses, students are reminded of the LI/SC. At the end of the lesson, it establishes criteria to assess.	Use the LI/SCs in the mini lesson, discussion at the end of the lesson. Reveal success criteria in multiple ways not only repeating what is posted, i.e., rubrics, models, student work, paraphrasing. Confer with students using the language of the SC.	Repeat LI/SC after the teacher. Students use LI/SC language as they are working with each other on the lesson and during share time.	SC posted and referenced. (For example: I can statements, student work, anchor charts, rubrics, etc.) Written feedback from the administrator.
Students are able to use the language of the learning intention and success criteria throughout the lesson.	Students using the language of LI/SC enhances their learning and responsibility for their own learning. Allows students to assess their own learning. Teacher moving throughout the room offering feedback and checking for understanding.	Using talk moves (repeating, revoicing, turn & talk, wait time, reasoning). Assessing student understanding based on the language of the LI/SC.	The students refer to the LI/SC during share time to explain their thinking. Students restate in their own words. Students using academic vocabulary. Student discourse using LI/SC in partners/groups. More student talk, less teacher talk.	High percent proficient on Daily Formative Assessments (DFA). LI/SC posted in a place/ position where the students can see and refer to them.

Once the team has had a chance to have rich dialogue around the look fors, they are given a rating scale similar to the one found in Figure 3.5 so they can self-assess how near or far they are from institutionalizing these practices in their classroom. Once each member of the team has a chance to rate themselves on each look for, a discussion ensues allowing each member to share their individual rankings. The team then comes to a consensus about where they want to concentrate their learning. For example, using the example found in Figure 3.5 this team rated themselves lowest on "students are able to use the language of the learning intention and success criteria throughout the lesson." This became the focus for the team's learning.

FIGURE 3.5. UNPACKING LOOK FORS ORGANIZER

1	2	3	4	5
Look for would never be found in my classroom.	Look for would rarely be found in my classroom.	Look for would sometimes be found in my classroom.	Look for would frequently be found in my classroom.	Look for would be found daily in my classroom.

After the focus is identified, the team develops one to two actions that help them improve their practice in this area. The team that identified their focus as "students are able to use the language of the learning intention and success criteria throughout the lesson" decided to work on questions, cues, or prompts that could be used during instruction that would bring students' attention back to learning intentions. The team spent time learning more about this topic.

The final steps are to implement and reflect. In our example, the team scripted questions, prompts, and cues related to their learning intentions and success criteria. They used these in the classroom and then brought student work to the PLC meeting to analyze the percentage of students who were proficient. During implementation the principal conducts focused walk-throughs providing feedback on specific look fors and action steps the team decided to use. In our example, the principal provided feedback on the use of teachers' questions, cues, and prompts and how responsive students were when probed about learning intentions and success criteria.

Teams stick with their focus for as long as it takes for them to see a positive impact on students. For some teams, this may be a few weeks; for others, it may be a month. A good rule of thumb is when 80 percent of the students show proficiency it is time to move on. This process promotes differentiation because teams are able to determine their area of emphasis and to move at a pace that is based on their students' progress. This also helps a leader differentiate individual support. If one teacher's student results are discrepant from other teachers on the team, it may be an indication that frequency of observations needs to be increased and/or it might be time to kick into the Element IV process.

Plan for Process and Content Learning

Making learning stick for adult learners requires a heavy emphasis on creating meaning. We want teachers to be able to think metacognitively about *what* they are teaching and *how* they are teaching so they can discern *when* the what (content) and how (process) will have maximum impact. If we want learning to transfer to classroom practice—and we do—then a commitment must be made to developing core knowledge on both teaching and learning. Teachers need time to think deeply about their own learning. Coupling knowledge and thinking increases the likelihood that learning will be actively applied in the classroom. This requires an "and" mindset when organizing professional learning. Spending exorbitant amounts of time on learning how to use a new textbook or on a discrete instructional strategy, practices utilized far too often in schools, won't help realize the goal of professional learning—impacting student outcomes.

Addressing both content and process learning necessitates a focus on curriculum. Standards and curriculum guides developed by the district office are useful, but what is *essential* is that teachers use these tools to make meaning about what students know and determine how to respond. Spending time unpacking unit standards (content) and then developing learning progressions (process) provides teachers with a clearer sense of both what and how to teach. Armed with this knowledge, common assignments and rubrics can be developed to analyze student work. The leader supports by noticing where teachers may need more professional learning and feedback

EQUITY CHECK

"Jointly examining student work reveals teacher thinking and provides a mechanism for inequitable practices to surface."

Creating an equitable school environment for all students regardless of race, religion, ability, gender, or sexual orientation requires more than wishful thinking and rhetoric. It requires the hands-on, side-by-side deep learning that occurs when principals and teachers work together to uncover the challenging issues associated with teaching students with diverse needs. This level of collaboration is necessary to uncover teachers' beliefs and misconceptions about how students learn. The practices in this element are designed to help teachers see how their actions positively, or negatively, impact student results. Jointly examining student work reveals teacher thinking and provides a mechanism for inequitable practices to surface. The principal's active engagement on these teams ensures that these issues can be addressed. The emphasis on actionable feedback promotes changes in behavior, which in turn can lead to changes in thinking (Sinek, 2015). It's about noticing and emphasizing what matters to benefit *all* children.

FROM THE FIELD

At Issue: Gail attended weekly PLC meetings with the math department. She noticed that the team needed to work toward a common goal aligned with the curriculum. Additionally, she noticed that achievement on the team was not growing and scores varied between individual teachers. It was time to focus and work with this team to improve.

The grade-level team from Chapters 1 and 2 was focused on the school improvement strategy of writing quality learning intentions and success criteria. Additionally, they were working to align targets with student work and provide feedback to students which utilized the language of the intention. Gail worked closely with the team to unpack standards so they would develop an understanding of what was needed to help students think deeply around important concepts. The team wrote learning progressions describing proficient student behaviors. They identified common misconceptions that would provide touchstones for the teacher to guide learners who were approaching the standard. Finally, they collaboratively wrote common formative assessments to measure progress and support next steps within a unit of study. Gail and the team would also use evidence collected by Gail during observations to analyze effective teaching strategies that seemed to be working in their classrooms.

All this work was done within the procedures and guiding principles of a PLC. They used questions like the following:

- What is it I want students to know? (unpacking of standards)

- What strategies will be most effective in helping students to learn the content? (microteaching)

- How will I know when students have learned the concepts? (common formative assessment)

- How will we react when students have learned? How will we react when students may not have learned? (analysis of student work)

The team began to see the value of working closely together. Their lessons were taught in alignment but with each individual working to put their own "spin" or voice into the mix. However, as the year progressed, Gail noticed that one teacher, Monica, was not seeing the same results as the other two teachers on the team. Gail met with Monica and together they decided to uncover the mystery as to why her students were lagging behind the other sections. Gail began going into Monica's classroom more frequently to get a better sense of what was happening. After three observations within a period of 2 weeks, a pattern began to emerge. When the two met, Gail began the feedback conversation with reinforcement for what Monica was doing well. Specifically, she told her that the learning intentions were clear and well written. Additionally, the success criteria supporting the learning were listed. However, while Monica was indeed using the language of the learning intention and success criteria, she was over scaffolding. She used the language too often and didn't allow students to do the thinking. She jumped in and gave them the answer or asked questions that did the cognitive work for the students. Gail used specific examples, and together they role-played scenarios. She gave specific feedback around over-scaffolding and coached Monica to wait. They brainstormed questions that would allow for open-ended thinking. When Monica felt that she understood the expectation, Gail went back and observed. Monica's students began to show tremendous progress. Daily formative assessment found her students to be "catching up" with the other classes. When the summative assessment rolled around, there were no differences in achievement between her students and her team. In fact, her scores were the highest for both her team and the entire district. The use of Element II supervision practices provided the specific and relevant feedback that allowed this team and each individual teacher to excel.

 Key Takeaways

Providing equitable and effective instruction for all students requires leaders to have a laser-like focus on both student and teacher growth. This happens when leaders embed collaborative structures into the culture of the school. To implement this, be sure the following occurs:

- Collaborative structures are embedded into the culture of the school.
- Focused walkthroughs and qualitative feedback are used to help teams and individuals improve practices.
- Student work is at the center of collaboration and decision-making so student needs are front and center.
- Support to teachers is differentiated based on student needs.

Like the perennial garden that endures and grows over time, the practices found in Element II of the differentiated supervision model help to sustain and promote lasting change. The deliberate time and attention spent in classrooms, working in teams, and examining student work sow the seeds for improvement and yield improved results.

WHERE ARE YOU NOW?

Leveraging group learning so all team members grow is a proven way to develop collective capacity. The following questions serve as a guide to promote reflection and prompt action as you develop your talents in helping lift all team members.

Getting started

Practices firmly in place

Planting seeds

Blooming

Knowledge	I understand that for teachers to think metacognitively about what and how they are teaching professional learning needs to include both content and process learning.	
	I have studied PLCs and what makes them work and what makes them fail. I revisit this information on a regular basis.	
	I understand the importance of and how to use student work during collaboration.	
	I continue to develop my own knowledge so I can provide relevant and meaningful feedback to teachers.	
Skills	When I note differences between PLCs, I adjust learning to meet the group's specific needs.	
	I use a focused walkthrough to help get a deeper sense of the issues that surface during observations or team meetings so I can help support teachers.	
	I have a structure for PLCs that includes identifying clear outcomes and uses a recursive action planning process.	
	I provide teams and individuals with feedback that leads to action.	
	I connect the focused walkthrough to the work in the other elements.	
Follow Through	I make attending and participating in PLCs a priority and rarely miss them.	
	Our teams make decisions based on student evidence.	
	I have developed tools to organize feedback and monitor progress.	

CHAPTER 4

· ·

ELEMENT III

Universal Support With Quantitative Feedback

"Gardens where plants, soil, and sunlight interact in a symbiotic way are breathtaking, and so are schools where human, social, and decisional capital interact seamlessly."

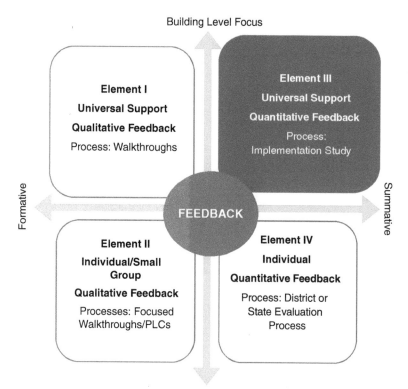

Building Level Focus

Formative

Element I
Universal Support
Qualitative Feedback
Process: Walkthroughs

Element III
Universal Support
Quantitative Feedback
Process:
Implementation Study

FEEDBACK

Summative

Element II
Individual/Small Group
Qualitative Feedback
Processes: Focused Walkthroughs/PLCs

Element IV
Individual
Quantitative Feedback
Process: District or State Evaluation Process

Classroom Level Focus

"**E**xecution is everything," a familiar mantra in the business world, is one that we ascribe to as well. If we want every child to have a quality teacher, it takes more than talk, it takes action. It's easy for schools to get caught up in the rhetoric of "continuous improvement" and confuse this with movement. A fierce, disciplined commitment to getting better requires a relentless focus on knowing what's working and what isn't, and then doing something about it. The unending cycle of adoption and abandonment without ever knowing the impact in classrooms results in mediocrity or worse. Excellence demands concentrated execution on practices that are making a difference.

Focused execution doesn't happen without a keen sense of the lay of the land. Knowing which practices are thriving and which aren't helps the leader know which seeds to sow. The work in this element provides the leader with a big picture look at how well teachers are executing the strategies in the school improvement plan and their impact, not for judgment's sake, but in order to identify what additional supports teachers may need. The practices in this element help to realize one of the promises of supervision, quality assurance.

CLARIFYING THE MODEL

Focus: School

The purpose for this element can be summed up in the quote from Ann's mentor, Nancy Mooney, "The work is not done until 100% of the students have benefited from the innovation." This element provides a summative check that helps the leader diagnose current implementation efforts. With this solid data in hand, leaders can make an educated decision about areas that need more professional learning. It also provides an opportunity to reflect on how near or far the school is in meeting school goals.

> *An implementation study is a scheduled visit to all classrooms in order to collect quantitative data on the execution of strategies in the school improvement plan.*

The primary process used in this element is the implementation study.

The function of the implementation study is to gauge progress, much like we do when we conduct benchmark assessments with our students. Unlike Elements I and II where qualitative information is collected, this process is simply looking for the presence or absence of look fors in the classroom which is why a checklist is being used. Rather than waiting until the end of the season to determine growth, this process provides intermittent checks so supports can be delivered when needed. Figure 4.1 outlines the steps in an implementation study.

FIGURE 4.1 IMPLEMENTATION STUDY STEPS

PROCESS	PURPOSE
Develop checklist based on look fors	Clearly defines what is being observed
Identify a 2-to-3-week period where data will be collected	Ensures that implementation study will be thorough and completed
Observe and collect data	Follow through with the commitment to SIP and ensuring all students have opportunities to learn
Share implementation data with entire staff	Creates time and space for conversations with staff about beliefs and practices
Analyze implementation data coupled with achievement data to determine next steps	Promotes collaborative problem-solving and continuous improvement

Assessment: Summative
Feedback Focus: Implementation Levels

The objective of this element is to quantify the progress the school is making on implementation of the school improvement plan. Feedback in this element is summative in nature, however formative in its use. A checklist is used to determine the presence or absence of look fors in classrooms which results in a percentage score. For example, the look for was observed in 15 out of 30 classrooms, resulting in 50% implementation. See Figure 4.2 for an example of an implementation checklist based on productive group work look fors. The data gathered from an implementation study provides feedback to the entire school, serving as a gauge that measures current progress. This feedback can then be leveraged to figure out what staff needs in order to improve implementation levels. Drilling down on the data by identifying the practices that are solidly in place and those that are flimsy or missing provides insights on what professional learning is needed next. Using data from the implementation study to drive professional learning makes learning more relevant to teachers because it's based on what was observed in classrooms and is firmly aligned with school goals.

Implementation study data provides opportunities for evidence-based dialogue, a necessary component of effective collaboration (Donohoo, 2021). Grappling with issues such as, "What helped ensure this practice was solidly in place?" and "Is there something we need to learn, do, or clarify to get more traction?" helps develop community and commitment. Teachers use the evidence from the study as both a celebration and a launching point for deeper learning.

FIGURE 4.2 IMPLEMENTATION CHECKLIST EXAMPLE

OBSERVED	NOT OBSERVED	LOOK FOR
		Group work is tied to the learning intentions from the focus lesson.
		Groups are formed via student choice and/or based on levels of needs from student need.
		Group work based on inquiry or problem-solving.
		Evidence of group accountability exists in tasks and assignments.
		Teacher monitors groups by using questions, cues, and prompts.
		Teacher is formatively assessing the group's product and the group's ability to work together.

WHY IT WORKS

Evaluative Mindframe

Many of us became school leaders because we wanted to maximize our impact across the school rather than in just one classroom. Maximizing impact isn't achieved by simply knowing about effective leadership practices.

Meaningful influence requires a way of thinking that aligns beliefs and practices in such a manner that produces positive results for students (Hattie & Smith, 2021).

In other words, it isn't enough to know what to do, leaders have to possess certain mindframes that help them understand why certain actions work better than others. The way school leaders think about their role helps to leverage impact on teachers, students, and parents.

One critical mindframe for leaders, according to Hattie and Smith (2021), is to evaluate their impact on teacher and student learning. This mindframe is central to the work of effective leadership because it, "highlights the capacity of educators to design effective programs informed by evidence, implement them with quality and fidelity, and then be able to critically determine the magnitude of the impact of their educational programs on student learning," (Clinton, 2021, p. 13). Leaders who possess this mindframe develop positive school cultures because they are always thinking and acting evaluatively, questioning what works and why, and encouraging others to do so as well. They create time and space for teachers to examine their impact and seek alternative views. They realize that collecting and analyzing data is a first step not an end unto itself. What really matters is the collaborative discussions about impact on students and teachers so the team can determine significance.

The essence of the work in this element of the differentiated supervision model is clearly driven by an evaluative mindframe. The implementation study embeds a process into the school that promotes data collection, questioning, and action into the fabric of how the school does its business, the epitome of evaluative thinking according to Baker and Bruner (2012). Taking this summative look periodically throughout the school year promotes evaluative thinking as it allows leaders to monitor program implementation and helps them see patterns across teachers and time frames so they can seek explanation via collaboration, allowing them to pursue alternative approaches if things aren't working (Clinton, 2021).

Quality Implementation

The good news is we know a lot about what works in schools, and we have for a long time (Hattie, 2009; Marzano, 2003). The not-so-good news is it is extremely challenging to get these practices firmly in place in a school. One reason it is so difficult is that incremental change isn't enough. Having a few teachers on board with initiatives won't move the needle on achievement. Student achievement increases only when a *majority* of teachers put practices in place (Reeves, 2008). Deep levels of implementation are required, and given the number and diversity of staff's beliefs and expertise, it is no wonder that this is difficult to achieve. Quality implementation, defined as "the process through which evidence-based promises of improvement-oriented interventions get realized into practice" (Donohoo & Katz, 2020, p. 5) must be the goal for school leaders.

However, achieving quality implementation is more nuanced than just a critical mass using practices. Scaling up educational change requires attention to depth, sustainability, spread, and shift in ownership of the reform (Coburn, 2003). Sustainability, according to Coburn, is the degree to which changes become ongoing habits of teachers and school practices. Depth refers to the deep and lasting learning of teachers and students. All of these factors require a transformational shift in educators' beliefs.

> *Lasting change, the essence of quality implementation, requires educators to wrestle with their thinking on what works and why so they can conclude that sometimes there are better ways to do things.*

This shift results in acceptance and ownership of evidence-based practices. Influencing this type of fundamental shift in a teacher's core beliefs takes more than simple collaboration. It requires engagement in progressive inquiry (Donohoo & Katz, 2020).

The process of progressive inquiry has educators using focused, goal-driven activities to improve areas of need and make changes based on feedback (Katz, Dack, & Malloy, 2018). Two distinct tactics of progressive inquiry methodologies include "monitoring and discussing activities or projects to learn from successful and failed initiatives and engaging in systemic analysis of data" (Katz, Earl, & Ben Jaafar, 2009, p. 73). The purpose of this process is to identify levels of implementation on specific aspects of a practice in order to reveal, through dialogue and data analysis, its current level of functioning. Through this exercise, beliefs are uncovered and can therefore be addressed. Teams are able to both deepen their knowledge and boost their confidence in effecting change.

Professional Capital: Focus on Decisional

When talking about improving schools, we ask principals to think of the ampersand symbol as a way to remind them that school leadership isn't about doing one thing in isolation, rather it is about connecting a series of practices in meaningful ways. Kim often says, "It's not one thing, it's *everything*." Hargreave and Fullan's (2012) professional capital framework supports this notion, asserting that leading learning requires equal measure and interaction of human, social, and decisional capital.

- Human capital, which has for too long been the focus of supervision, pertains to individual talent. Are there skilled teachers and principals in the system?

- Social capital refers to the quality and quantity of social interactions in schools. How often and how well do teachers and principals collaborate?

- Decisional capital is the ability to make good decisions and judgments based on experience and learning. How are decisions made when the answers aren't clear-cut?

When all three capitals are working together, both groups and individuals improve. Gardens where plants, soil, and sunlight interact in a symbiotic way are breathtaking, and so are schools where human, social, and decisional capital interact seamlessly.

Creating the conditions for professional capital to thrive requires deliberate attention. The differentiated supervision model works because all three capitals are addressed. Human and social capital are highlighted in the work of Elements I and II, while decisional capital takes center stage in Elements III and IV.

Decisional capital increases as the process for making decisions expands from the individual to the group. Collaborating over data from the implementation study promotes collective decision-making. Professional judgment becomes more powerful when the decision-making skills of individuals and groups work in tandem (Fullan, 2014). Having staff deliberate over implementation study results in order to identify next steps allows them to move beyond superficial participation, or tokenism, toward greater involvement and influence. This results in staff feeling more empowered and increases efficacy as they collectively problem-solve to overcome challenges (Donohoo, 2017).

MAKING IT HAPPEN

Infrastructure: Connect the Work

Infrastructure is the underlying foundation or basic framework of a system or organization. There are many moving parts within any infrastructure, and the strongest ones make sure there are definitive overlap and connectedness among these parts. Tightly interconnected systems help the organization maintain function and promote flexibility and responsiveness. When parts of the system don't work together, the system fails. What's hard is creating connected systems that can weather any storm.

Creating a schedule that connects supervision processes in a way that can withstand the disruptions inherent to schools is required.

> One of the aims of the differentiated supervision model is to help principals organize their time in a manageable way so they can support the main function of schools, student learning.

Building this connective system starts with the 3-week feedback cycle described in Chapter 1. After teachers are divided into a cycle and weeks are designated for observations, the principal needs to identify which weeks will include an implementation study. Remember implementation studies typically occur 2 to 3 times a year, once every 8 to 10 weeks. Figure 4.4 provides what one semester sample schedule would entail. All teachers are observed at a minimum once every 3 weeks. These observations don't stop during the weeks that an implementation study is being conducted as noted in Figure 4.3. The difference during these weeks is that the leader includes the checklist and upon entering the classroom checks off the look fors present.

There are a finite number of minutes in a day. As much as we feel the pressure for more time, it is unrealistic to waste our energy wishing for more. What we have to do is leverage the time we have. Coupling the implementation study with the regularly scheduled observations is like tilling the soil and planting seeds simultaneously. It also helps to maintain the weekly schedule and allows the leader to have consistent blocks of time when they aren't in classrooms so they can deal with issues that arise during the day.

FIGURE 4.3 OBSERVATION SCHEDULE

	TEACHERS		DATES	IMPLEMENTATION STUDY
Feedback Cycle Group 1	Mrs. A Mr. B Ms. C Ms. D Ms. E	Mr. F Mr. G Mr. H Ms. I. Mrs. J	First week of September	NA
Feedback Cycle Group 2	Mrs. K Mr. L Mr. M Ms. N Ms. O	Mrs. P Mrs. Q Mr. R Mr. S Mr. T	Second week of September	
Feedback Cycle Group 3	Mrs. U Mrs. V Mrs. W Mrs. X Mrs. Y	Mr. Z Ms. AA Mr. BB Mrs. CC Mr. DD	Third Week of September	
Feedback Cycle Group 1	Mrs. A Mr. B Ms. C Ms. D Ms. E	Mr. F Mr. G Mr. H Ms. I. Mrs. J	Fourth Week of September	NA
Feedback Cycle Group 2	Mrs. K Mr. L Mr. M Ms. N Ms. O	Mrs. P Mrs. Q Mr. R Mr. S Mr. T	First week of October	
Feedback Cycle Group 3	Mrs. U Mrs. V Mrs. W Mrs. X Mrs. Y	Mr. Z Ms. AA Mr. BB Mrs. CC Mr. DD	Second week of October	
Feedback Cycle Group 1	Mrs. A Mr. B Ms. C Ms. D Ms. E	Mr. F Mr. G Mr. H Ms. I. Mrs. J	Third week of October	NA
Feedback Cycle Group 2	Mrs. K Mr. L Mr. M Ms. N Ms. O	Mrs. P Mrs. Q Mr. R Mr. S Mr. T	Fourth week of October	
Feedback Cycle Group 3	Mrs. U Mrs. V Mrs. W Mrs. X Mrs. Y	Mr. Z Ms. AA Mr. BB Mrs. CC Mr. DD	First week of November	

	TEACHERS		DATES	IMPLEMENTATION STUDY
Feedback Cycle Group 1	Mrs. A Mr. B Ms. C Ms. D Ms. E	Mr. F Mr. G Mr. H Ms. I. Mrs. J	Second week of November	Implementation study-collect checklist data
Feedback Cycle Group 2	Mrs. K Mr. L Mr. M Ms. N Ms. O	Mrs. P Mrs. Q Mr. R Mr. S Mr. T	Third week of November	
Feedback Cycle Group 3	Mrs. U Mrs. V Mrs. W Mrs. X Mrs. Y	Mr. Z Ms. AA Mr. BB Mrs. CC Mr. DD	Fourth week of November	
Feedback Cycle Group 1	Mrs. A Mr. B Ms. C Ms. D Ms. E	Mr. F Mr. G Mr. H Ms. I. Mrs. J	First week of December	NA
Feedback Cycle Group 2	Mrs. K Mr. L Mr. M Ms. N Ms. O	Mrs. P Mrs. Q Mr. R Mr. S Mr. T	Second week of December	
Feedback Cycle Group 3	Mrs. U Mrs. V Mrs. W Mrs. X Mrs. Y	Mr. Z Ms. AA Mr. BB Mrs. CC Mr. DD	Third week of December	

Use Both Impact and Implementation Data

Improving a school isn't a linear endeavor; it is more of a series of starts and stops. One variable advances before another one can: The latter variable moves, while the former stays constant or declines (Elmore, 2008). What this means in practice is that substantial changes to instructional practice can occur in a school, but the external measures of performance may stay the same. Leaders must hypothesize, observe, investigate, and analyze information on changes in student learning throughout the year to guide day-to-day actions. Without this focus, leaders can interpret a lack of results on external measures to mean that the school isn't making progress and abandon practices that may actually be getting leverage. Abandoning practices too soon can have a catastrophic effect on both student achievement and the culture of the school, unwittingly stoking the "this too shall pass" mentality so common in continuous improvement discussions. The remedy to this is to, in the words of John Hattie, "know thy impact" for both achievement and implementation.

Monitoring both implementation and impact data answers two important questions: "Is the strategy being implemented at high levels?" and "Has implementation made a difference?" The implementation study is a key piece in answering the first question, and when coupled with achievement data can provide a comprehensive view of progress and challenges. Making this happen requires a leader to determine from the outset what data is going to be collected. Measures must be identified for the strategies in the school improvement plan that answer both questions. The focus is on school and grade-level or department data. Figure 4.4 provides an example of the implementation and impact data collected for a literacy strategy in a school improvement plan.

The dual analysis of data in the implementation study provides context and insights into next steps that a myopic look at data cannot deliver.

Tending to both implementation and impact data helps the leader unearth the root causes for results enabling a more precise response.

The implementation study data guides the use of other supervision processes such as the focused walkthrough. Consider this example from an elementary principal whose school had the goal of increasing proficiency in reading and math. The strategy identified to meet this goal was to implement learning targets and respond with appropriate instruction at the individual, small-group, and whole-group levels. Due to the complexity of the strategy and it being the beginning of

FIGURE 4.4 SIP IMPLEMENTATION AND IMPACT DATA EXAMPLE

Strategy: Use one-on-one conferring to respond to formative assessment results.	
Impact Data	• Common formative assessments used for each unit of study • Reading benchmark data • Student-centered coaching cycles pre/post results • Data wall placements (quarterly) • State assessment results (yearly)
Implementation Data	• Walkthrough data and feedback to staff members (weekly) • Average number of one-on-one conferences per student as observed during implementation study (2x per year) • Implementation study (3x per year) • Data dig results identifying mastered and unmastered standards

the school year, the principal decided to focus on the look for, "students can state the learning target of the lesson." Data indicated that students clearly understood learning targets for mathematics but had difficulty stating them during reading. Impact data from common assessments that measured standards showed limited mastery in reading, while again math data looked stronger. Armed with this information, the principal conducted focused walkthroughs during the reading block. These observations coupled with feedback and data analysis in PLCs revealed that teachers weren't monitoring and responding during small group instruction. Also, one-to-one conferring with students was rarely occurring, even though in the previous year staff had received considerable training on this. Knowing that students needed these supports, whole-group professional development time was used to help staff develop a deeper understanding of what guided practice and conferring should look like in literacy. From this learning, the staff co-constructed a restructured literacy block so richer opportunities for small groups and one-on-one instruction could occur. The combination of impact and implementation data positions the leader to be more efficient, accurate, and effective in making decisions, saving one of our most precious commodities, time.

Collaborate Using Results

One of the biggest benefits of the implementation study is that it creates time and space for conversations on the application of classroom initiatives. It's difficult, if not impossible, to determine if a new approach is making a difference if we don't have a sense of if and how it is being used (Hall & Hord, 2006). However, careful attention must be given to how discussions around implementation study data are conducted. Simply sending an email or sharing at a staff meeting that 52% of the staff are "modeling using a think aloud" isn't enough and squanders the opportunity for deep discussions around teachers' beliefs and practices.

One way to ensure that data conversations around implementation studies are meaningful is to create an environment where teachers feel safe to discuss both successes and failures. Mastery experiences, a key source of collective efficacy (Bandura, 1997), cannot be obtained in the absence of learning from failures or mistakes (Donohoo & Katz, 2020). Thus, leaders need to create processes that promote open-ended, thought-provoking questions, allowing teachers to share their ideas and opinions. We use a data analysis protocol for this work (Love, 2001). This can be done verbally or via writing (using Jamboard or other tools). Each round consists of answering questions privately, then sharing in small group, and finally large group discussion. What is critical is that every staff member gets a chance for their voice to be heard and that next steps are clearly identified and agreed upon. Figure 4.5 outlines the protocol process.

FIGURE 4.5 IMPLEMENTATION STUDY DATA ANALYSIS QUESTIONS

	ACTIVITY	PURPOSE
Round 1- Preview	Teachers answer the following prompts: • I predict implementation data will show . . . • I wonder . . . • My questions/expectations are influenced by . . . • Some possibilities about learning that this data may present . . .	Engages staff, helps to surface beliefs
Round 2- Review Data	Teachers review data and answer the following prompts: • Some patterns and trends that I see . . . • I am surprised that I see . . . • I believe this data suggests . . . because . . . • I am not surprised that I see . . . because . . .	Focuses on the data, helps to tease out big ideas from the information presented
Round 3- Individual Needs	Teachers answer the following prompts: • What I did to contribute to . . . • I am stuck on why/how to . . . • I would like more support in . . . • I think we should try . . .	Provides time for self-reflection
Round 4- Define Action	Teams share out needs and actions via what they need to stop doing and what they need to start doing. The group reaches consensus about next steps.	Promotes collective commitment

EQUITY CHECK

"The systems we create in our school can either promote or depress learning opportunities for our students."

It's common sense, backed by decades of research, that students need equitable opportunities to learn from challenging curriculum (Carroll, 1963; Tschannen-Moran & Hoy, 2000). When students are consistently assigned texts well below their grade level or assigned tasks that have little cognitive demand their opportunities to learn are stifled and achievement suffers. The good news is that as leaders, the opportunity to learn is something we can control. The systems we create in our school can either promote or depress learning opportunities for our students. Dismantling tracking systems, where lower-achieving students are stuck in low-level curriculum and courses, is a must, but simply grouping students heterogeneously or moving them into higher-level classes isn't enough if teachers' beliefs about their abilities to teach and students' abilities to learn don't shift.

Addressing equity in a system must include opportunities for teachers and teams to discuss beliefs that can help examine and adjust their expectations. Teachers' low expectations for students impact students' beliefs about their own abilities (Brophy, 1983). Whether a teacher, team, or student thinks they can or can't, they are right. Efficacy beliefs shape expectations and performance. Our job as leaders is to raise teachers' expectations of themselves and their students. We do this through building collective teacher efficacy—the shared beliefs that through teachers' combined efforts they can positively influence students' outcomes, including those of students who are disengaged, unmotivated, and/or disadvantaged (Donohoo, 2017). Efficacious teachers and teams have high expectations stemming from their beliefs they can face any challenge. Building this resilience in teams requires the type of mastery experiences that are provided in all aspects of the differentiated supervision model but are elevated in this element. The implementation study process provides teachers with a chance to monitor progress toward collective goals utilizing open to learning conversations to determine what is working and what needs to be refined. This process coupled with the tools in previous chapters helps teachers and teams wrestle with their beliefs and practices in a manner that helps them set and meet high expectations for themselves and their students.

FROM THE FIELD

At Issue: The plan was in place. The team collaborated and developed a clear strategy and action steps that they felt would change outcomes for students. After several weeks of implementation, Principal Gail noticed that the strategy wasn't having an impact on achievement. Gail had to figure out what was in the way.

The initial work was done. The SIP team had looked at data and determined their school improvement strategy would be to implement quality learning intentions and success criteria. Specifically, the team decided to focus on writing, teaching, and assessing students using learning targets and success criteria. The staff had engaged in learning via whole staff and small group opportunities and had collaboratively developed clear look fors. After 6 weeks of implementing learning targets and success criteria, Gail decided it was time to do an implementation study using the look fors as follows:

Writing/Use

- Learning targets are written, posted, and stated with clarity in student-friendly language.

- Learning targets reflect what will be learned in the lesson.

- Success criteria are written with specific language that breaks down the learning and provides benchmarks for quality.

- Success criteria have one of the following: is used as a rubric, has a bulleted list, or has a description or a model.

Assessing Student Work

- Teachers use the language of the learning target/intention and success criteria through prompts, cues, and questions (scaffolding to learn vs. scaffolding to complete).

- Feedback focuses on the success criteria and is based on specific standard(s) and performance.

    o Qualities of work; Unravels misconceptions (What am I trying to learn?)

    o Refers to benchmarks for the learning (How much progress?)

    o Advice for the future (Where to next?)

- Students use the language of the success criteria to monitor or self-assess their progress.

After observing in all classrooms, Gail took a look at the data. It was clear to her that the majority of her staff were writing and using learning targets and success criteria. However, the data confirmed what Gail had been noticing during general walkthroughs and PLC meetings, too many students were well below proficiency targets for this point in the year. Gail's hypothesis was that too much teacher scaffolding and talk was being used so students weren't getting a chance to show what they knew during independent work. However, she knew she couldn't confirm this assumption until staff had a chance to review and discuss the data.

Armed with achievement and implementation study data, Gail used the protocol found in Figure 4.5. This process uncovered that teachers still didn't have a deep enough understanding of how to use the learning targets and success criteria with students. They could write and post but lacked understanding of how to assess students and adjust instruction. Teachers shared things like, "I want to really support my students so they understand" or "I am not sure they can do the work without my support." The teachers decided that more study was needed on how to minimize whole group teacher talk and maximize teacher-to-student interactions. They decided to focus on the look for around questions, cues, and prompts.

Gail and the leadership team got busy on providing professional learning around questions, cues, and prompts. Staff was given time to read, reflect, and implement new understandings. PLCs used student work to monitor the impact this change was having on achievement. All the while Gail was providing support in PLCs and focused feedback on this aspect of instruction.

After several months of concentration, Gail decided it was time for another implementation study. Her focus was on using the look fors on assessing student work. She found that the work was paying off—more teachers were implementing at high levels which also showed up in student data. More students were moving to higher levels of proficiency. When staff had a chance to reflect on this data, they shared that they felt they had a better sense of what students could and couldn't do, which in turn helped them shift their instruction. Staff celebrated this progress but knew there would be more studies and data to analyze in the future!

 **Key Takeaways**

Hope is not a plan. Hope can move people to do great things but only when accompanied by action. We can't hope our way into wanting all students to have high-quality instruction. We have to connect the expectation of obtainment (the definition of hope) with behaviors and actions that turn desire into reality. To implement this be sure to do the following:

- Have a clear sense of where you are headed, where you are now, and where to go next.

- Use the real-time information from the implementation study to make collective decisions about next steps.

- Be transparent with data so staff can collectively wrestle with what is happening, sharing understandings and beliefs.

- Identify next steps collaboratively, providing staff with a voice in the process, upping both ownership and the likelihood of quality implementation.

Contrary to what the nursery rhyme tells us, it isn't silver bells and cockleshells that make a garden grow; it is careful planning and ongoing attention to the health of the plants. Student growth requires this same meticulous scrutiny.

WHERE ARE YOU NOW?

Monitoring and responding to a school's progress on implementing school improvement initiatives is necessary when building collective capacity. Use the questions below to help you gauge where you are in making this happen.

Getting started — Practices firmly in place

Planting seeds — Blooming

Knowledge	I understand that quality implementation is more than just a compilation of practices that it requires educators to wrestle with what works and why.
	I embrace the importance of transparency and share all implementation study data with all staff so we can engage in rich dialogue.
	I realize the need to compile and analyze both impact (student achievement) and implementation data in order to make sound decisions.
Skills	I use protocols when sharing data to help ensure all staff voices are heard.
	I work with teachers to analyze data and revise professional development that support the growth and development of all teachers.
	I can have meaningful conversations around the implications of the implementation study.
	I connect implementation studies to the work in the other elements.
Follow Through	I conduct implementation studies 3 times a year using a checklist based on look fors.
	I revise and adapt based on the needs of the staff.

CHAPTER 5

· ·

ELEMENT IV
Individual Support With Quantitative Feedback

"The growing season is over in the garden, and it's time to recognize the bounty from a year's worth of work. It's time to answer the question: 'How has your garden grown?'"

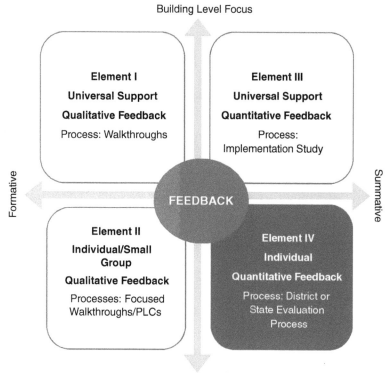

Building Level Focus

Element I
Universal Support
Qualitative Feedback
Process: Walkthroughs

Element III
Universal Support
Quantitative Feedback
Process:
Implementation Study

Formative

FEEDBACK

Summative

Element II
Individual/Small Group
Qualitative Feedback
Processes: Focused Walkthroughs/PLCs

Element IV
Individual
Quantitative Feedback
Process: District or State Evaluation Process

Classroom Level Focus

Most of us would like to think of ourselves as skeptical of unsubstantiated claims, irrational ideas, and silly theories. We don't fall for the ad that tells us this one pill will melt off the weight or cure all of our aches and pains. We understand that there is no one easy quick fix to solving complex issues like health and wellness. And yet we succumb to this mentality when it comes to supervision. The formal evaluation process has been established, embraced, and exalted as the "miracle grow" for helping teachers improve. Despite the time and energy given to the process, this methodology continues to produce lackluster results. In part, we lean in this direction because it appears like the straightforward answer. Improved teaching equals improved learning. However, as stated previously, schools are a complex system and as such require more nuanced solutions. Just as getting healthy requires more than taking a daily pill and plants need more than fertilizer to bloom, it takes more than a formal evaluation to help a school meet achievement outcomes.

Individualistic approaches like formal evaluations don't work because they become an end in and of themselves. They aren't productive because they don't influence the culture in the way that focused collaborative work can (Fullan, 2014). Hopefully we have established that supervision is an ongoing process embedded in the day-to-day work of the school.

> The differentiated supervision model includes formal evaluation but contextualizes its impact by placing it within a system of improvement.

In other words, evaluation isn't the sole driver, it works alongside and with the other methods providing a connected solution. The work in this element ensures the formal evaluation process is maximized by attaching to the other systems of the differentiated supervision model.

CLARIFYING THE MODEL

Focus: Individual

Most districts design formal appraisal systems to provide feedback about the teacher's performance during episodes of teaching. Formal evaluation processes vary from district to district, but the typical format consists of some general goal setting meetings at the beginning of the year and then 2 to 3 rounds of observation cycles that include 1) a preconference where the teacher and principal discuss what will be observed in the upcoming lesson; 2) an observation on a mutually agreed upon date, usually 45 minutes to an hour in length; and 3) a postconference meeting to discuss what the leader observed and fill out the mandated district forms. The differentiated supervision model isn't about stopping this process—we don't want you to lose your job. However, it is about upending the why and how.

In the differentiated supervision model, the formal evaluation process is used to provide feedback on current practice so teachers can expand their repertoire of teaching skills and enhance their intellectual growth. Borrowing from both Cognitive Coaching (Costa & Garmston, 2016) and Clinical Supervision (Goldhammer, 1969), the formal appraisal process is used as an opportunity to engage in dialogue that supports the complex cognitive task of examining and improving teaching practice. Leaders use a continuum of interactions from consultant (let me explain how), to collaborator (let's brainstorm ways how we can), and coach (what do you think) to help teachers think through and improve teaching practices.

The distinct lens used for the phases of formal evaluation is compared to traditional methods in Figure 5.1. Rather than treating formal evaluation as an event that is "done to" a teacher, differentiated supervision treats the process as something "done with" the teacher that builds on previous conversations and feedback. This shifts the process from a "gotcha" to a "helpya" approach.

FIGURE 5.1 COMPARISON OF FORMAL EVALUATION PHASES

PHASE	TRADITIONAL MODEL	DIFFERENTIATED SUPERVISION MODEL
Goal Setting		
Teacher's Role	• Review teaching standards • Identify one to two areas of focus for the year	• Reflect on past practice • Share evidence of areas of strength and student data • Ask probing questions that help determine goals for the year • Seek principal's input
Leader's Role	• Ensure goals are clear and measurable • Evidence to support goal attainment clearly articulated	• Listen to the teacher • Ask probing questions around evidence to help teacher focus on strengths and areas for growth • Ensure goals align with school improvement and district targets • Connect teaching standards to the teacher's goal
Preconference		
Teacher's Role	• Mentally rehearse and orally discuss upcoming lesson • Submit lesson plan that includes all components of instructional model	• Share learning targets and success criteria for the lesson • Reflect and revise instructional strategies aligned to goals that the teacher has been working on that will be observed in the lesson • Seek input on lesson as needed

(Continued)

FIGURE 5.1 (CONTINUED)

PHASE	TRADITIONAL MODEL	DIFFERENTIATED SUPERVISION MODEL
Leader's Role	• Seek clarity on what the teacher has planned for the lesson • Ask probing and clarifying questions	• Promote reflection by reminding teacher of feedback that has already been shared via walkthroughs, both general and focused • Share ideas as needed to ensure lesson is designed for success
Observation		
Teacher's Role	• Teach the lesson as planned and as well as possible • Fend off anxiety	• Teach the lesson • If not going as planned, change and revise based on student's response due to a comfortability with being observed
Leader's Role	• Script events of what is happening during the observation as accurately as possible	• Observe and take anecdotal notes as needed • Talk to students about their learning • Look for evidence of learning intention and success criteria • Generate questions to be used during postconference based on what is observed
Postconference		
Teacher's Role	• Share perspective on areas that went well and areas that improved • Receive feedback	• Reflect on the lesson by sharing success criteria and evidence/examples of which were met and which still need work • Ask questions • Collaborate with the leader on next steps
Leader's Role	• Gather teachers' perspectives of the lesson • Share feedback based on state teaching standards	• Collaboratively review evidence of success criteria with the teacher • Ask probing questions • Develop a plan of action with timelines

Assessment: Summative

Feedback Focus: Differentiate

Differentiated supervision is designed to match the level of support with the needs and competencies of individuals. This occurs in all aspects of the model but is extremely explicit in the approach to feedback for this element. All teachers need feedback to improve, but not all feedback will have an impact if the approach is one size fits all. Determining what a teacher needs requires a leader to know both what needs to be improved or refined and a clear sense of which approach will lead to the greatest likelihood that the teacher will act on the feedback. Fertilizer doesn't take unless the conditions are optimal and neither does feedback. Coupling types of feedback (Hattie and Timperley, 2007) with Cognitive Coaching stances, as outlined in Figure 5.2, is the approach used in the differentiated supervision model.

FIGURE 5.2 TYPES OF FEEDBACK AND COACHING STANCES

FEEDBACK TYPE	NEEDED WHEN	COACHING STANCE	SENTENCE STARTERS	WHAT IT SOUNDS LIKE
Task	Teachers learning something new. Teachers have limited experience using or understanding.	Consultant	Pay attention to . . . You should . . . It's important that . . . Always keep in mind . . .	"When sharing today's learning intention, you turned your back to the students and didn't include success criteria. This was very confusing to your students. It's important that learning intentions be tied to success criteria, otherwise students won't be able to monitor their learning. Let's review what success criteria entails." "You should be aware of who you are engaging with during class. Two students answered questions during your lesson. Five students were disengaged. Let's review other methods of engaging students."
Process	Teachers are at surface-level implementation. Student results are not at desired levels or are surprising.	Collaborator	Let's examine . . . How might this affect . . . ? What are you thinking . . . ?	"Students had difficulty comparing and contrasting. Why do you think this happened? Let's examine the depth of knowledge for the task to help us figure out what happened?" "Students were attentive during your lesson. How could you increase student talk about learning? How might this affect independent work?"
Self-Regulation	Teachers are aware of what works. They recognize results are reflected and are in alignment with teaching.	Coach	What might be some ways to . . . ? What are additional possibilities. . . . ? How do you know it worked . . . ? What would you change about . . . ? Why?	"What do you think you did during this lesson that worked, what are your plans for the students who didn't reach mastery?" "What would you change about how you organized student groups during instruction?"

Task Feedback

Task feedback is information focused and leads to acquiring more or different information. This type of feedback, also called corrective feedback, is the type that may be used most frequently with new teachers or when teachers haven't acquired the skills they need to implement a new teaching practice. This feedback is explicit and direct, so a consultant stance is the best approach to delivering feedback. In the consultant stance, the leader transfers information about procedures or professional practice, focusing on the what and whys. This feedback is instructive in nature, putting the leader in teacher mode as they provide direct guidance.

Process Feedback

While task feedback is designed to help acquire learning, process feedback is aimed at deepening learning. This feedback helps teachers process information by engaging in dialogue about what is working, what isn't, and why. This helps teachers rethink approaches and detect where more effective methods would be warranted. This feedback is most useful when trying to get teachers beyond surface levels of implementation. Asking probing questions, examining classroom evidence, and helping define the problem are part of the collaborative stance that the leader takes when using this type of feedback.

Self-Regulation Feedback

The approach used when delivering self-regulation feedback is that of a coach. This posture works because this feedback is designed to promote self-reflection. Supporting teachers in knowing which students are progressing and which need support, while helping them work through self-identified issues with their practice, is the aim of this feedback. Teachers who are continually trying to improve their practice are most receptive to this type of feedback. Many times, we shy away from providing feedback to those "rockstar" teachers for fear we can't help them improve. However, when these teachers are given feedback that helps them reflect and self-assess, they flourish. This coaching stance requires an inquiry-focused approach so that the teacher can self-evaluate, developing a conscious awareness of what makes a difference with their students.

A Delicate Balance

As much as we advocate for coupling feedback types with coaching stances, these practices can't be completely compartmentalized. For example, a new teacher may need both task feedback as well as process and self-regulation. In one conference, both task and process feedback may be required. And as the leader, you will need to adjust your coaching stance both within and between conversations.

The key is knowing when to water and when to fertilize, and this is dependent upon a level of intimacy with the conditions needed for growth. It is why the work in the other elements is so critical. Without frequent classroom observations, working alongside a teacher in PLCs, and providing ongoing feedback, it is difficult if not impossible to know and understand what the teacher needs in a summative situation.

> The level of teacher experience, new or veteran, cannot be the sole determinant for deciding which types of feedback to use. It must be aligned with teachers' needs.

WHY IT WORKS

Learning Is Emphasized

As previously stated, formal teacher appraisal instruments are blunt and rarely lead to improved outcomes for students.

Relationships are strengthened and trust is developed when teachers and principals work together, doing the collective work of improving teaching and learning (Robinson, 2011). This type of work builds relational trust because the focus isn't on judging how weak or strong a teacher might be, but the supports needed to improve. Teacher evaluation scales simply don't improve student performance, in part because the process unwittingly promotes a one-dimensional episodic approach to improvement. What improves student performance is a culture where learning is embedded into the day-to-day work of the school.

> *What works are collaborative cultures where teachers and leaders have established high levels of trust by using feedback for growth and being transparent about results (Fullan, 2014).*

The differentiated supervision model doesn't lead with the teacher evaluation process. The model's focus is on creating a culture of learning through work in the other elements. The principal's time and energy are spent working alongside teachers providing timely and focused feedback. This model puts this process in its appropriate place, as a supporting player to the larger work of school improvement. Gardeners don't organize their work based on the tools in their shed, how silly. It is just as irrational when we use the formal evaluation process as the driver to improving teacher quality. The focus is on cultivating a system where everyone learns and grows together.

Connecting Formative and Summative Measures

One of the central aims of the differentiated supervision model is to help teachers improve the complex work of teaching and learning. This requires a leader to be skilled at providing feedback that answers both "What are the next steps in learning?" and "What has been achieved to date?" Teachers confronted with these same questions for student learning rely on both formative and summative assessment data to make decisions. Formative assessment feedback tackles next-step-sized learning targets; summative measures are concerned with medium-term goals for achievement over a period of time such as a semester or year.

Both formative and summative data are necessary to make good decisions. Take for example the teacher looking to increase math achievement in her class. She knows from state assessment results that math problem-solving skills were low but relies on daily work and other measures of formative assessment to craft lessons. The state data helps identify an area of concern, but in order to pinpoint students' needs, additional formative information is necessary. Using data to reason and make decisions requires a two-step process (Brookhardt, 2016). First, determining areas of need, and secondly determining why this is occurring. Summative data helps identify strengths and areas of need while formative data helps determine what steps need to be taken to address issues. Coupled together a more complete and accurate response can be crafted to support student learning.

Connecting formative and summative assessment data shouldn't be limited to classroom practice. In the differentiated supervision model, formative and summative data is linked so the leader and teacher can identify next steps in the learning journey, while also documenting progress. Summative data may show that a teacher's growth rates for students in below basic and basic categories were stronger than students in average or high ranges. A review of formative data from walkthroughs throughout the year can help distinguish what practices might be making this occur.

Frequency of Feedback

Feedback's importance in the improvement process makes logical sense. If we want to get better at something that matters, we need information on how we are doing. Feedback bolsters progress because it makes us more knowledgeable about our performance. When we work hard at something and are successful, it is inherently motivating (Pink, 2009). That's the power of feedback; not only can we get better, but we will also *want* to get better. We can't get better at something if we only hear about it once or twice a year. Timely and specific feedback is critical to improved performance. Positive comments help build confidence while constructive feedback clarifies expectations and allows people to learn from their mistakes.

96% of employees, according to Pink's research (2009), report they want regular feedback.

Nestled in the center of the differentiated supervision model is feedback. It takes a central role because it has the potential to transform performance for teachers and students. The connectivity between the processes in all four elements ensures that feedback unfolds throughout the year preventing the annual performance review from becoming a meaningless compliance check.

MAKING IT HAPPEN

Infrastructure: Utilize Tools From Other Elements

One of the benefits of using the differentiated supervision model is that it makes the formal evaluation process more efficient. Evidence from general and focused walkthroughs gives the leader a heightened understanding of the teacher's repertoire of skills both before and after the "formal" observation. The principal is privy to the body of the teacher's work rather than a few short snapshots. Connecting the formal evaluation process to the informal process provides a more realistic picture, leading to a more authentic conversation and feedback. This also helps reduce time spent on determining a focus for the observation as well as developing the post write-up.

Leveraging these benefits requires the principal to go back into the feedback log and walkthrough summary form and review the teacher's progress over the course of the year. Making this information useful is dependent upon the amount of analysis and reflection on the part of the school leader. We have found that color coding is useful in helping patterns emerge. For example, if the SIP strategy is to implement focus lessons, we might highlight the cells red when learning intentions and success criteria were mentioned, yellow when modeling was present, and green when checks for understanding were included. Analyzing which colors are present and which are missing helps the leader identify areas of strength and need. Sharing this with the teacher during the preobservation conference allows the teacher and leader to use concrete evidence to collaboratively determine areas of focus and set goals.

Earlier we mentioned that we should "back in the teaching standards." The feedback log and focused walkthrough summary tools provide a mechanism to make this happen. Earmarking which standard and which indicator were mostly present during the observation allows the standards that are firmly in place to emerge allowing the leader to authentically connect teaching strengths and standards. The key here is to connect this rich data to the formal process. In doing this, the leader leverages the observation process so it is rooted in realistic evidence shaped from the unique needs of the teacher.

Pay Attention to the Supervision Conference

Making mid-year/end-of-the-year evaluation conferences meaningful requires principals to deliberately link observations to school goals and the aligned professional learning that has been occurring through the methods found in the other elements. This anchors the work and provides context for rich conversations. The postobservation conversation moves out of alignment when it is dominated by talk about each of the district-established criteria for teacher evaluation. This results in an evaluative potpourri of suggestions, observations, reinforcements, and questions that leave a teacher with little useful feedback. In the differentiated supervision model, postobservation conferences align with the blueprint processes for school improvement, building on further improvement of teaching and student learning that has been established during previous conversations.

> Don't treat this conversation as an isolated event; use past learning and previous feedback to help shape dialogue and inquiry throughout the exchange.

The supervision conversation needs to be designed so that the teacher sees how their efforts align with the mission, beliefs, values, and goals for the school. In this way, neither principals nor teachers become overwhelmed attempting to implement or monitor too broad a spectrum of outcomes. This doesn't happen when the feedback is driven by the broad teaching standards developed by states and districts. A structure that helps the leader plan the conference, connecting previous work while using inquiry and self-reflection, is what is needed to make the postobservation conference productive.

We advocate for a framework adapted by Mooney and Mausbach (2008) and found in Figure 5.3 that provides a skeletal outline from which principals can shape preparation for the conference. This structure keeps the conversation focused while also allowing for flexibility to meet a variety of conference goals. Teaching standards are identified but are not the driver for the conversation. We like to say that we "back in" the standards, connecting them to the specifics of what was observed.

The framework for a postobservation conversation is easily modified to accommodate a variety of supervisory situations. Principals need to focus on improving teaching, not fixing a lesson that has already been taught and cannot be recaptured. The more serious the difficulties with teaching, the more directive the principal's role as described in the feedback section of this chapter. Reflection and self-assessment are always the ultimate goal as the ability to self-assess marks maturity and greatly increases the chances of growth beyond the confines of the postobservation conversation.

Create a Teacher Map

One of the challenges in providing differentiated supports to individual teachers is getting a grasp on the level of support needed when there are

FIGURE 5.3 SUPERVISION CONFERENCE FRAMEWORK

CONFERENCE PHASE	PURPOSE/DESCRIPTION
Introduction	Start with an introduction that is cordial, sincere, and relational. This shouldn't be a greeting that quickly turns to the heavy content of analyzing a teaching episode. An effective introduction fosters the climate of trust and respect necessary for an effective conference.
Reflection & Information Gathering	Listening is key here. A time for reflection and information gathering allows the supervisor to fill in the blanks from the observation by listening to the teacher's perspective on strengths and challenges. It is an important time for teacher reflection fostered by skillful questioning and listening. The principal uses this time to pay attention to what the teacher already believes is needed to improve teaching—not tell the teacher what they think. To achieve this, the principal must ask focused questions to foster reflection and listen intently for the insights of the teacher. This helps the leader complete their diagnosis and check if inferences made about teaching practices are valid. Using inquiry to find out why the teacher made certain instructional decisions helps leaders shape more accurate feedback that reinforces good practices and refine those that need work.
Reinforcement - Strengths	During this portion of the conference, the principal points out strengths both observed and those that were shared as part of the teacher's reflective process. The purpose of this phase is to cement effective teaching behaviors. Keep this list short (no more than 2) so teachers can remember it, and make sure it is specific. Select one or two that have the greatest influence on learning or support implementation of professional development efforts. Use this part of the conversation to build on strengths.
Check for Understanding	Throughout the conference, the principal assures that the teacher's understanding of the conference content matches that of the principal. The principal asks the teacher to rephrase the big ideas regarding strengths—making this sound conversational rather than a pop quiz. Skipping this step is detrimental because without it the principal and teacher may leave the conference with different perspectives.
Refinement - Improvement	Improving teaching requires confronting what needs improving. Effective conferences use teacher reflection or principal findings that have the greatest chance of influencing student learning. Identifying too many refinements or being vague about the need for improvement defeats the purpose of this part of the conference.
Check for Understanding	See "Check for Understanding" section above.
Summary Statements	The conference concludes with summary statements for closure. Typically forms for documenting the conference are shared or signed. Next steps, including a timeline for future actions, naturally emerge in this closing phase of the conversation.

several teachers to supervise. How does a leader get their arms around what can feel like an enormous task? One method we have found to be useful is to create a map based on levels of support a teacher might need. Three areas are examined: achievement, learning environment, and levels of implementation of SIP strategies. Putting this information in one spot helps the leader identify both individual and building needs. While we believe wholeheartedly in teacher collaboration and input, leaders need mechanisms that help them manage the complex work in front of them. Without these processes, leaders can't organize the work, and effective collaboration becomes more difficult. This is one method tailored to helping the leader do the cognitive work around teacher supervision. Figure 5.4 provides an example of a teacher map. In this example, it is clear that Mr. F is in more urgent need of more support than Mrs. H and Ms. Ch. After reviewing teacher data, the principal can determine which area of supervision would have the greatest leverage point. For Mr. F. this might be learning more effective classroom procedures and routines.

We recommend that mapping should occur 3 times a year and most definitely at the end of the year so the leader can plan for and adjust supports. Remember monitoring happens throughout the year as observations are ongoing. The key to using this tool, just like using a data wall for students, isn't about

FIGURE 5.4 TEACHER MAP

TEACHER NAME	AVERAGE PERCENT GROWTH ON MAP	PERCENT PROFICIENT DISTRICT ASSESSMENT	LEARNING ENVIRONMENT	SIP IMPLEMENTATION
Mrs. H	+80%	90%	Some behavior referrals and has intermittent control of the classroom. Students inconsistently engaged.	Preponderance of look fors present during observations and implementation study.
Mr. F	48%	75%	Multiple behavior referrals and shows lack of classroom management and student engagement.	Few if any look fors present during observations and implementation study.
Ms. Ch	60%	73%	Few referrals. Students consistently show evidence of engagement and can explain how classroom procedures work.	Some look fors present during observations and implementation study.

categorizing teachers, it's about what *actions* the leader takes after this type of analysis. A variety of actions can be taken based on this data. For example, a leader might want to increase the number of observations and feedback for teachers. Providing professional learning for a small group of teachers who are lagging in SIP implementation would be another appropriate strategy. Tapping on teachers who are doing well so they can share during small-group learning would also be useful. The bottom line here is that this data isn't about sorting, it is about helping the leader reflect on the individual teacher's strengths and needs and then doing something to address what surfaces. We don't recommend using this process if a leader isn't committed to using it as a method that provides guidance and insight into helping teachers grow.

EQUITY CHECK

"Equity requires telling the truth about a teacher's current level of achievement and then working alongside them to support improved practice."

The desire for equity can be seen in the statements "all children will succeed" or "every individual will reach their potential" espoused in mission statements plastered around schools. Making this a reality requires more than posters and slogans. It takes intentional actions. A starting point for school leaders is to think differently about supervision and in particular the formal evaluation process. The hyper-focus on ensuring the process is fair has put an emphasis on filling out forms and checking boxes. This homogenization unwittingly contributes to promoting an inequitable system because teachers' needs, just like students' needs, vary. Equity requires telling the truth about a teacher's current level of achievement and then working alongside them to support improved practice. Meeting teachers where they are and helping them grow is the way they find the path forward for their students. For leaders who truly desire an equitable school, it is imperative that we address teacher quality head-on. This doesn't happen by using a one-dimensional evaluation system that at its best is perfunctory and at its worst meaningless. The methods found in the differentiated supervision model augment the formal evaluation system, ensuring that the feedback teachers receive throughout the year is acted upon. This focused intentionality is an important starting point for making sure all students get what they need.

FROM THE FIELD

At Issue: Gail knew that evaluation of teachers using a one-time-per-year approach had very little effect on achievement. She knew that she had worked hard and collected data on every teacher and wanted to use it to support summative teacher assessments.

Gail believed that as the principal she wore two very distinct hats. The first hat is the baseball cap of a coach. She wore this hat a lot as she worked alongside teachers helping to improve their practice while building trusting, safe relationships. The second hat Gail wore was the fedora of the evaluator. While she didn't wear this hat as often as the baseball cap, she knew her teachers needed summative information that would help them reflect and grow. Her goal was to establish relevant feedback conversations based on the formative data she collected all year while also using the district's evaluation tool.

She knew she could leave nothing to chance, so at the beginning of the year she started to think about how to connect the work in the other elements to the summative evaluation process. She set up structures that she would use to gather formative data during her informal walkthroughs; these tools included the feedback journal, walkthrough summary, and teacher map. This initial step was the foundation for the year as it helped her stay organized as she went through her feedback cycles. These three tools provided a way for her to collect data in an efficient and effective way. With these structures in place, Gail asked each teacher to provide the times during the day that they preferred feedback. Allowing teachers to decide when they wanted to discuss observations helped to establish trust and routine so the ongoing feedback that occurred every 3 weeks was timely and relevant.

Once the logistics were in place, Gail knew that she would need to establish a mindset that set the stage for the formal evaluation process. She provided professional development around the teaching standards and the district evaluation process. She then engaged in collaborative conversations with each teacher to establish their goals for the year. Her goal was providing teachers with enough support so that they could eventually identify the standards reflected in their work. She explained how observations would be scheduled not as one-time events but embedded into the feedback cycles. This provided structure so teachers would consistently know "where they stood" in relation to set standards of teaching practice while maintaining the integrity of the district evaluation process. The formal observations included preconferences, observations, and postconferences. This data also went into the teacher spreadsheet for review throughout the year.

These organizational tools guided Gail's work throughout the school year. She was flexible in how she used them and was consistent in providing feedback to each teacher. When the time came to complete the summative evaluation using the district forms, she simply looked at her data from the walkthrough log and summary and had a quality conversation with the teacher. Because she had shared the information throughout the year, the things discussed weren't a surprise to the teacher. It was a collaborative conversation based on relational trust. The conference used student results and observations to reinforce teacher practices that were on target. She asked the teacher reflective questions allowing them to take an active role so they could clearly articulate their teaching strengths. She also used the data to help the teacher refine and set goals for future practice. She continued to use reflective questions so the teacher was clear on what could be done to improve. This structure wasn't foreign as it was identical to the process used throughout the year when informal feedback conversations occurred.

Teachers reported that they felt empowered and that the evaluation process was relevant to their teaching. They didn't feel insecure, but were confident in what they accomplished and how they would refine practice in the future. Gail knew this system was effective and made the difference because she had clear data to support the improvements made throughout the school. She used the individual feedback provided throughout the year as a means to change the entire school. The results were strong, and achievement was on the move. Teachers knew their work helped to create a culture of learning and morale was high. Gail was glad she wore both hats and stayed consistent.

Key Takeaways

The growing season is over in the garden, and it's time to recognize the bounty from a year's worth of work. The plan from the beginning was to create a space that would produce and sustain growth. It's time to answer the question: "How has your garden grown?" To answer this question be sure to do the following:

- Focus on individual teacher practice using formative and summative measures.

- Use the plethora of evidence generated from the other elements of the differentiated supervision model.

- Create a culture where teachers take an active role in the evaluation process, empowering them to reflect on what is working and identify where they want to continue to grow.

WHERE ARE YOU NOW?

The formal evaluation process is the most impactful when it is linked to ongoing feedback from the other elements. For this to be effective, a leader has to pay deliberate attention to connecting the work. Use the statements below to rate how near or far you are to making this happen.

Knowledge	I have a deep understanding of my district/state's teaching standards.
	I am aware of the need to use various coaching stances during supervisory conversations.
	I understand the four types of feedback and when each is most effective.
Skills	I connect formative observations and feedback to the summative evaluation.
	I connect the district evaluation system to the work in the other elements.
	I plan for supervisory conferences and have a structure in place for conducting them.
Follow Through	I developed an infrastructure that supports ongoing data collection for individual teachers and staff.
	I have tools to analyze teachers' current levels of performance.

CHAPTER 6

· ·

LEADING THE DIFFERENTIATED SUPERVISION MODEL

"But like the little gardener, leaders must persist. The practices in the differentiated supervision model, when put in the hands of a skillful leader, plant seeds of excellence."

Helping everyone in a system grow and develop is no small task. We have used the analogy of a garden throughout this book because for us it best illustrates the care, intentionality, and connectedness inherent to system growth. Tending to the diverse needs of the adults and students in a school requires the same type of meticulous attention plants need to thrive. The differentiated supervision model provides a framework, serving as the lattice for growth and development. However, it takes a skilled and committed leader for the structures and supports to thrive and make a difference. Consider the following two scenarios, keeping an eye on the leadership behaviors in both examples.

PRINCIPAL A

Principal A is hardworking and respected by staff and colleagues throughout the district. She actively participates in district-provided professional development with her teachers and takes this back to her school, working with instructional coaches to ensure staff learning is engaging and fun. She has worked with staff to develop a focused school improvement plan, and annually, staff collaborate on developing look fors on the strategies in the plan. She conducts general walkthroughs on a regular basis and is religious about attending professional learning communities. During PLCs, considerable time is spent sorting student work into three piles: proficient, basic, and below basic.

(Continued)

(Continued)

She is timely in providing feedback to staff, typically in the form of a note or email. Her feedback is brief, typically including a look for that was present and encouragement to keep up the good work. She conducts at least one implementation study a year, sharing data with staff afterward, making sure to celebrate when they are over 60% implementation. Her formal evaluations for teachers are always completed on time, spending considerable time making sure that teachers receive feedback on each of the district standards. She is able to accomplish this by using a "cheat sheet" of phrases that are easy to plug in to the forms as needed.

Achievement for Principal A's school fluctuates from year to year. A high percentage of students remain in the low-performing growth categories on local and state measures. Student growth at the advanced levels of achievement is flat. Staff satisfaction ratings of the principal remain high, yet teachers still report feeling overwhelmed and misunderstood. Student achievement is not showing steady gains.

PRINCIPAL B

Principal B is also hardworking and respected by staff and colleagues throughout the district. She actively participates in district-provided professional development with her teachers. Before adopting district professional learning into her school, Principal B sits down with her leadership team to discuss which aspects of this learning align with their current data and school improvement plan (SIP) to determine if and how this could help meet their goals. Once the team outlines their thinking, it is shared with the entire faculty for input so the SIP can be updated. Before committing to SIP strategies, the staff make sure to check on effect size to ensure that the strategy is high leverage enough to move achievement. With the plan updated, Principal B and her staff collaboratively develop look fors.

Principal B uses the language of the look fors to provide feedback to staff after general walkthroughs, in PLCs, and in one-on-one face-to-face meetings after observations. She frequently consults her considerable professional development library when providing feedback to staff to ensure that it includes "why this matters," upping the likelihood of deeper implementation. She analyzes her feedback frequently to identify patterns and trends in implementation efforts. She uses this analysis to help refine professional learning and is not afraid to seek out new learning when the data isn't making sense to her. She is constantly checking on impact by having teams scrutinize student work and analyze growth data so discrepancies in student learning can be addressed. Staff collaborate on specific ways to attend to students' needs, leaving PLCs with a clear plan to move forward. Principal B encourages staff to revisit what worked and what didn't after implementation and is an active participant during the collaborative inquiry process.

Her staff reexamine look fors after a few months to make sure they reflect their continued learning and insights from implementation. Implementation studies are conducted twice a year. Staff review implementation study data, coupled with student achievement data, to adjust their practices and update/revise the school improvement and professional development plan. Data from the walkthroughs conducted throughout the year serve as the basis for individual formal evaluations. Principal B aligns what has been observed all year to the teaching standards and works with the teacher to identify areas of strength and areas of growth.

Achievement for Principal B's school is showing steady gains. Students in the low-performing growth categories on local and state measures are decreasing and the advanced levels are increasing. Staff satisfaction ratings of the principal are high, and staff openly acknowledge that they are responsible for the positive changes in the building and see a correlation between their work and the impact it has on their students. Student achievement is showing steady gains.

LEADERSHIP BEHAVIORS AND THE DIIE MODEL

Even though both principals use the same processes, there is a clear distinction between these two leaders that explains the variance in student outcomes. The difference comes down to some nuanced leadership behaviors. Principal A's approach is superficial, leading with a "check the box" mentality. Principal B uses a recursive cycle of diagnose, intervene, implement, and evaluate (DIIE) (Hattie & Smith, 2021). These somewhat subtle but critical differences in the leaders' approaches are what sets these two apart. A side-by-side comparison is found in Figure 6.1 in order to help understand the variation in the two approaches.

FIGURE 6.1 LEADERSHIP COMPARISON

LEADERSHIP BEHAVIOR	PRINCIPAL A NON-EXAMPLE	PRINCIPAL B EXAMPLE
Diagnose: understanding how students are performing from multiple evidence-informed contexts in order to better support teachers	Relies on the district initiative without analyzing student data. Sees feedback as a task, doesn't use it to help discern what is working and what isn't.	Examines student data to determine best approach to district-level initiatives. Analyzes feedback frequently to look for patterns and trends.
Intervene: knowing what strategies or interventions have the most probability for success and knowing when to switch	Feedback is more focused on frequency than providing insight into instructional practice. Feedback is superficial and lacks relevance. Lacks an emphasis on using student work in PLCs to identify how to intervene next.	Ensures that feedback aligns with the current knowledge base. Actively engages in PLCs to determine what is working and what isn't. Seeks out discrepancies in the data to determine next steps. When stuck, networks and/or researches to find solutions.
Implement: committing to fidelity in quality of delivery and duration	Focuses on quantity, not quality, during implementation study. Lacks a clear goal that focuses on change. Data is not used transparently nor analyzed in meaningful ways.	Revisits look fors to help staff get clarity and achieve quality implementation. Uses the implementation study to adjust practices across the school. Revises professional development plan to meet goals. Celebrates growth with staff. Sees the connection between implementation and impact.
Evaluate: using multiple methods of evaluation of effectiveness	Infrequent dives into the data and what it means. Approaches evaluation with an emphasis on compliance. Focus is on making sure each standard is addressed rather than helping teachers reflect based on their practice. Formal evaluation process is done to the teacher.	Constantly checking on impact by looking at data. Aligns the formal evaluation to feedback received throughout the year. Formal evaluation process is collaborative with the teacher.

HOW BEHAVIORS ALIGN TO ELEMENTS I, II, AND III

Diagnosis: According to the dictionary, diagnosis means a thorough analysis of facts or problems in order to gain understanding and aid future planning. When leaders engage in the activities in all the elements—but particularly Elements I, II, and III—a rich analysis of performance, from multiple perspectives, is developed. Leaders who engage in the processes and constantly ask themselves what is working, what isn't, and why, will find the model the most effective. Principal B separates herself from Principal A by connecting the processes and continually trying to make meaning out of what she sees and hears both in classrooms and in student data. This principal is hyper-focused on using the data around her to better understand and meet the needs of teachers and the school. She has a vision of what her school will become and how to make that happen.

Intervention: Two important things must happen for leaders to be skilled at intervening. First, they must possess relevant knowledge. Robinson (2011) defines this as "up-to-date, evidence-based knowledge of how students learn and of how teaching promotes that learning in diverse classroom contexts" (p. 23). Knowledge in the areas of content, pedagogy, curriculum, and how students learn is necessary. Without this know-how, it is difficult, if not impossible, to provide feedback that is rich and meaningful. Principal B understood that and consulted professional readings to ensure that feedback supported the teacher in thinking deeper about how to sustain or improve practice.

The second quality leaders need when it comes to intervention is the ability to discern which strategies are having an impact, which aren't, and then having the courage to do something about it either way. School leaders must nurture an environment that focuses on interventions that have a high probability of success and develop a collective mindset that if students aren't successful it's because the right teaching intervention hasn't been found *yet*. Principal B is open to making necessary changes when expectations for the student are too low and puts a high value on working collaboratively with staff to determine if interventions are successful.

Implementation: Leaders who have expertise in implementation are firmly committed to fidelity. Ensuring that school improvement strategies are being used and supporting teachers in quality implementation is a strong tenant of this model. Conducting the work in Element III and connecting what is learned to Elements I and II not only increases the likelihood of quality implementation but shapes professional learning in meaningful ways. Implementation study data served as a checkpoint for Principal B, helping her discern what future learning staff needed so they could reliably implement strategies, which led to positive growth for students.

Evaluation: Leaders who have skill in evaluating are able to judge significance using multiple measures. They are constantly judging progress to determine if actions are making a difference. A consistent mantra of "so what?" drives them to assess impact. The cognitive process involved in answering that question helps them to engage in rich evaluative thinking.

Element IV

When it comes to the formal evaluation process, the power lies in helping teachers engage in this same type of thinking. Skilled leaders help teachers use evidence collected throughout the year to identify strengths and weaknesses so the process becomes more about engagement and less about compliance. Connecting the informal processes conducted throughout the year, as seen with Principal B, provides a multitude of data and a broad lens on the scope of the teacher's work. From this wide-ranging vantage point, the leader works alongside the teacher to help evaluate how they made a difference. The process is transparent, the teacher owns the outcomes, and they aren't surprised by the conversation.

> *The differentiated supervision model has the biggest impact when a leader commits to engaging in thinking that has them continuously analyzing the data around them, intervening appropriately, focusing on quality implementation, and evaluating the difference.*

The differentiated supervision model sets up a framework that can promote DIIE thinking in a way that permeates the daily actions of a school leader. However, as witnessed with Principal A, the tools and processes will fall flat if the school leader fails to dig deep and simply goes through the motions.

DO THIS, NOT THAT

We have long been fans of those simple books found in the healthy living section of bookstores that tell you to "Eat This, Not That." We like the uncomplicated advice because it serves as a reminder of how to apply what we know about healthy living. In that same vein, we have identified some guidance that will help you put the DIIE mindframe into practice as you implement the differentiated supervision model (Figure 6.2).

LEADERSHIP COMMITMENTS

In the introduction, we shared three critical commitments that stem from the principle that the purpose of schooling is student learning. They are 1) implementing school improvement processes at a high level, 2) developing a school culture that promotes learning, and 3) using a growth mindset to develop and enhance professional capital. Keeping these commitments at the forefront of the work helps the leader uphold the mission of schooling, allowing them to engage in DIIE behaviors around the critically important work.

The commitments stem from the professional capital equation discussed throughout the book. According to Hargreaves and Fullan (2012), capital refers to "one's own or a group's worth, particularly concerning assets that can be leveraged to accomplish desired goals" (p. 1). It's a basic business principle that for capital to grow investments need to be made in assets.

FIGURE 6.2 DO THIS, NOT THAT

	DO THIS	NOT THAT
Overall	*Seek Connectedness* One of the questions a leader should continually pose as part of their evaluative mindframe is, "Does this action, decision, feedback, etc. connect or fragment the work?" The tools and processes in the model are designed to promote connectivity. However, without a leader's deliberate attention, supervision can become disjointed and siloed. Keeping it connected requires the leader to make intentional connections to the work and learning in all of the elements.	*Leave Staff Behind* Supervision, to be effective, is not something that can be done to staff. We repeat, it cannot be done *to* staff. Thus, from the get-go, leaders have to keep staff informed and engaged in the process. Helping staff see the connections between your general walkthroughs, work in team meetings, and implementation studies is paramount to helping them understand the what and why of supervision.
Element I	*Take Time to Think* Far too many times principals fall prey to working the structure (i.e., filling out a checklist or rubric) without understanding what was observed and how to follow up. It can be motivating to stand in the back of the room and provide immediate feedback to the teacher during a walkthrough (one less thing to do when you get back to your office!). But in our haste, we shortchange the opportunity to think and reflect on what was seen and how it connects to previous observations. Making sense of what we observe in classrooms and PLCs requires real consideration as teaching and learning is a complex endeavor. When we push on without thoughtful deliberation, we aren't able to diagnose, and our feedback becomes cursory and meaningless.	*Be Stagnant About Your Own Learning* This almost seems so obvious that we didn't include it, but this is too important to be left to chance. If we want to influence both the students and teachers in our care, then we need a depth of understanding on both teaching (effective pedagogy) and learning (how students master new information). The work in this element focuses on implementing initiatives that impact the entire school. Knowing what initiatives have the greatest impact in terms of student learning is mandatory for a school leader. This requires keeping current by carving out time to learn.
Element II	*Emphasize "Yet"* The work in this element centers on examining student work. While this can be rewarding when we see students' progress, it can also be extremely frustrating when we don't and even more defeating when we don't understand why. Emphasizing "yet" at this juncture, when the team or individual is in the thick of it, helps not only diffuse emotions but can open up thinking on how to intervene next. Statements such as "Results aren't what we want yet" or "We haven't tried ____ yet" should become an integral part of the leader's vernacular.	*Forget the Power of Good Questions* As leaders we sometimes fall into the trap of thinking we need all of the answers, when in reality the opposite is true. What we need to have at the ready is a set of good questions. And to get good at questioning we have to have context. This means knowing what is happening in classrooms and having a firm grasp on how to analyze student data. Thus, during team or one-on-one meetings besides actively listening, the leader can ask open-ended questions that help everyone dig deeper so effective interventions can be identified.

(Continued)

FIGURE 6.2 (CONTINUED)

	DO THIS	NOT THAT
Element III	*Be Relentless About Finding Evidence* The benefit of the work in this element is that it provides a picture of the present level of functioning. With this in hand, the school team can take a ruthless look at reality in order to identify what's next. The pitfall is that sometimes it can be difficult to clearly see what's in front of us. Not because we don't want to see, but because we are so invested in the work it's difficult to take an objective look. Being hyper-focused on finding evidence of the specific criteria for the implementation study coupled with distinct achievement targets helps the leader both when determining quality implementation and designing intervention.	*Confuse Implementation With Understanding* Schools and school systems are full of good soldiers. Good soldiers are those people that support the district or school by implementing initiatives even when they don't understand the value or purpose in doing so. The problem with a preponderance of people with this attitude is that many times their compliance masks misconceptions they have and if left unchecked over time fosters resentment and confusion. Checking for understanding through face-to-face discussions and frequent observations are critical in order to determine levels of understanding, helping to identify how to improve implementation efforts.
Element IV	*Listen to Help Diagnose* One of the greatest aids in our work with teachers is our ears, and no time is this more important than during the summative conference that is central to this element. Allowing the teacher to do the talking and thinking provides the leader with valuable insight. Listening helps the leader discern if the teacher is consciously competent and in what ways, helping the leader diagnose next best steps.	*Take All the Air Time* To borrow a phrase from the musical *Wicked*, the purpose of the work in this element is to help the teacher "be changed for good." The most impactful way to do this is to allow the teacher to look at the evidence collected throughout the year and have them reflect and identify their effect.

Teachers are one of our greatest assets. Their professional work, capacity, and effectiveness deserve a lot of our attention. Investing in professional capital—the combination of human, social, and decisional capital—needs to be of utmost importance (Hargreaves & Fullan, 2012). When these capitals work in tandem, they have the power to transform teaching and learning. Upholding these commitments provides a leader with a clear avenue for making sure all three capitals are addressed and developed. The moves identified in the "Making It Happen" section of each of the previous chapters contribute to asset development. The differentiated supervision model is powerful because it harnesses professional capital, ensuring that we get the best return on our investment—improved student achievement.

IT'S YOUR TIME

Ann's mentor always reminded her that there is not one right starting point: The only wrong thing you can do is not to take that first step. As you reflect on where to begin with the differentiated supervision model, we encourage you to do a self-inventory of the practices that you may already be using. Once you have those identified, the challenge becomes integrating them into this comprehensive model in a connected way. We have provided a summary of the reflective statements from the building capacity section of each chapter in Appendix C so you can take a holistic look at your current status. Couple this information with what you know about your staff so you can decide the starting point that makes the most sense for your current situation.

FINAL THOUGHTS

The children's book *The Little Gardener* (Hughes, 2015) tells the story of a boy who is frustrated and overwhelmed with the enormity of caring for his garden. He loves the garden, it means the world to him, but he gets discouraged by his small size and how much work needs to be done to make it thrive. However, he persists, and one plant blooms giving hope to others who are motivated and start to grow. In the end, the plants work together with the little boy creating a beautiful and wondrous garden.

Leaders who implement the differentiated supervision model may encounter the same frustrations and joys as the boy from our children's story. It is easy to get overwhelmed by the enormity of caring for and nurturing a whole school or school system of students. Leaders can feel small and inconsequential in their attempts to make improvements and support students and staff. But like the little gardener, leaders must persist. The practices in the differentiated supervision model, when put in the hands of a skillful leader, plant seeds of excellence. Working together in service of student learning, leaders and teachers are inspired to provide the kind of care that everyone in the school deserves. The result will be a bountiful harvest of student growth. What can be more satisfying than that?

APPENDIX A
Differentiated Supervision Timeline

Summer	• Conduct a leadership retreat to help support SIP planning • Divide teachers into 3-week cycles for observations • Create feedback journal, walkthrough summary, and teacher map documents
Fall To-Dos: → Develop SIP → Develop professional development plan → Collaboratively develop look fors → Conduct implementation study in late fall	**Monthly:** • Meet with leadership team to analyze data and review school improvement • Update teacher map

	Weekly:
	• Conduct general walkthroughs and provide feedback
	  ○ Analyze feedback journal
	  ○ Update walkthrough summary
	• Observe and meet with new staff
	• Participate with PLC
	  ○ Establish norms and protocols
	  ○ Review purpose and provide professional learning regarding PLC/learning teams

Winter To-Dos: → Review and revise SIP based on data → Monitor professional development plan → Conduct implementation study → Revise look fors based on implementation data	**Monthly:** • Meet with leadership team to analyze data and review school improvement • Update teacher map • Conduct observations to comply with district appraisal system

	Weekly:
	• Conduct focused walkthroughs and provide feedback with designated staff
	• Conduct general walkthroughs and provide feedback
	• Analyze feedback journal
	• Update walkthrough summary
	  ○ Observe and meet with new staff
	  ○ Participate with PLC
	• Analyze student work
	• Develop response to student data
	• Monitor effectiveness of PLC as related to look fors and student data (PLC self-assessment)

Spring To-Dos:	Monthly:
→ Review and revise SIP based on data → Monitor professional development plan → Conduct implementation study → Revise look fors based on implementation data → Conduct summative evaluations → Identify and celebrate progress	• Meet with leadership team to analyze data and review school improvement and update for upcoming year • Utilize teacher map for summative evaluation • Conduct observations to comply with district appraisal system

	Weekly:
	• Conduct focused walkthroughs and provide feedback with designated staff
	• Conduct general walkthroughs and provide feedback
	  ○ Analyze feedback journal
	  ○ Update walkthrough summary
	• Participate with PLC
	  ○ Analyze student work
	  ○ Develop response to student data
	  ○ Monitor effectiveness of PLC as related to look fors and student data (PLC self-assessment)

APPENDIX B

Example School Improvement and Professional Development Plan
ABC School

School Improvement and Professional Development Plan 2020–21

MISSION: ABC School is committed to providing exemplary education through a rigorous and engaging curriculum that meets the needs of the whole child.

CORE VALUES: We believe in:

- cultivating a school climate that values relationships.
- supporting our students to high academic achievement.
- creating a road map toward graduation that considers the individual needs of students.
- fostering a passion for lifelong learning.

School Leadership Team Members (list): One teacher from each grade level is represented on the team as well as a special education teacher and the school counselor. Our leadership team commits to cultivating trust, supporting a coherent vision, and empowering *all* with a purpose to build collective efficacy, advocate for children, and *advance achievement*.

OVERVIEW
Culture

- Consistent Building-Wide Instructional Discipline Model: Referral and suspension data shows higher rates in the last few years. One way to prevent this could be a uniform PD on a specific research-based Instructional Discipline model and implementation of advisement daily.

- Average daily attendance less than 95%. Chronic absenteeism 18% (students missing more than 10% of the school year).

- Teachers need to utilize restorative practices and staff need to do first interventions in the classroom rather than pulling the student from instruction. The correlation between access to the learning center for disruption and cool down is directly aligned to referral data. This data needs to be utilized to develop Tiers 2 and 3 interventions.

Academic

- High variance teacher to teacher in all subject areas, i.e., Math 46%–82%, Reading Comprehension 52%–77%, and Science 48%–82%. This may indicate a need to discuss expectations, quality of learning intentions/success criteria, and systemic response to data collected.

- MAP data indicates higher percentages of students in low and low average bands. Teachers will need a focus on growth and utilize this data throughout the school year.

- Evidence indicates teachers will need a focus on implementing the Building Blocks of Universal Tier, particularly Assessment for Learning and Instructional Practices.

GOAL I

LIST GOAL

By May of 2021, students' reading and math achievement will improve as measured by 80% of students meeting expected growth on the MAP assessment.

STRATEGIES

STRATEGY	EVIDENCE OF STRATEGY IMPLEMENTATION (HOW WILL YOU KNOW THE STRATEGY HAS BEEN IMPLEMENTED)
Teachers will implement a literacy and math workshop with an emphasis on writing and utilizing clear learning intentions and success criteria.	Written, posted use of learning intention and success criteria. Teachers providing feedback based on learning intention/success criteria. Implementation study will indicate that 80% of teachers are implementing the components of the workshop.

ACTION STEPS

KEY: I = Initiate, P = Progressing, M = Met, C = Canceled

Strategy A: Teachers will write learning intentions and success criteria in the literacy and math workshop and respond to students based on success criteria.

ACTION STEPS #	ACTION STEPS TO IMPLEMENT STRATEGY:	PERSON RESPONSIBLE	I	P	M	C
1	Using the text *Teacher Clarity Playbook* teachers will learn to write quality learning intentions in literacy.	Staff and Administrators	x			
2	Teachers will examine student work using specific protocols.	Individual Classroom Teachers		x		
3	Using the text *Challenging Learning Through Feedback* teachers will implement and analyze the effect their feedback has on student work.	Individual Classroom Teachers	x			
4	Teachers will utilize learning intentions/ success criteria in every component of the workshop (mini-lesson, guided, collaborative, independent, close).	Individual Classroom Teachers	x			
5	Teachers study, analyze, and utilize MAP benchmark data, student work, and common formative measures.	PLC		x		
6	Conduct implementation study 3 times/ year (pre/monitor/post assess). Utilize revised look fors weekly feedback.	Administrators		x		

GOAL II

LIST GOAL

By May of 2021, student attendance will increase to 97% (average daily attendance) and the number of students that miss 10% (chronic absentee) or more of their school year will be reduced by 50%.

STRATEGY	EVIDENCE OF STRATEGY IMPLEMENTATION (HOW WILL YOU KNOW THE STRATEGY HAS BEEN IMPLEMENTED)
Implement a system of advisement in every classroom.	Decrease in the number of referrals. Increase in average daily attendance. With 80% fidelity, 100% of the teachers will be utilizing *effective advisement activities* as measured on the look for document.

ACTION STEPS

Strategy A: Implement a system of advisement in every classroom.

KEY: I = Initiate, P = Progressing, M = Met, C = Canceled

ACTION STEPS #	ACTION STEPS TO IMPLEMENT STRATEGY:	PERSON RESPONSIBLE	I	P	M	C
1	Advisement team will revise and develop the advisory framework, expectations, look fors, and monitoring form.	Advisement Group, Administrators		x		
2	Create a schoolwide social norming campaign to improve attendance, behavior, and self-regulation.	Counselors, Staff	x			
3	Staff will participate in professional development that identifies strategies to improve attendance, behavior (using tier 1, 2, and 3 interventions), and self-regulation skills.	Staff	x			
4	Utilize data collected from the advisement monitoring form, Olweus Bullying Questionnaire, Panorama, and other available tools for teachers to confer with students.	Teachers, Administrators, Staff		x		
5	Rotate leadership roles during meetings to build collective efficacy within the multidisciplinary team.	Leadership Team		x		
6	Conduct implementation studies to monitor culture goals.	Administrators		x		

PROFESSIONAL DEVELOPMENT PLAN

Part I: Outcomes

By the end of the year, our staff will be able to know/do:

	OUTCOMES	GOAL/ STRATEGY
1	Write quality learning intentions and success criteria in every component of the workshop (100% of teachers, 80% fidelity).	Goal 1 Strategy 1
2	Provide actionable feedback to every student in their classroom.	Goal 1 Strategy 1
3	Implement advisement framework 3 days a week.	Goal 1 Strategy 1

Part II: The Plan

DATE	DESCRIPTION OF LEARNING ACTIVITY	HOW (PLC TIME, LARGE GROUP, EARLY RELEASE, ETC.)	OUTCOME LIST
Sept.–Oct.	Read *Teacher Clarity Playbook* and complete activities	PLC	1
Sept. (Week 1)	School improvement overview develop look fors	Large group	1–3
Sept. (Week 2)	Components of advisement	Large group	3
Sept. (Week 3)	Components of workshop overview math	Large group	1–2
Sept. (Week 4)	Components of workshop overview literacy	Large group	1–2
Oct. (Week 1)	Data walk	Large group	1–3
Oct. (Week 2)	Introduction to the social norming campaign	Large group	3
Oct. (Week 3)	The focus lesson use of learning intention/ success criteria math workshop	Large group	1
Oct. (Week 4)	The mini-lesson use of learning intention/ success criteria literacy workshop	Large group	1
Nov. (Week 1)	Write learning intentions/success criteria using student work	PLC	1
Nov. (Week 1)	SIP benchmark data and implementation study review	Large group	1–3
Nov. (Week 2)	Advisement strategies and share	Large group	3
Nov. (Week 3)	Guided groups and the use of learning intention/ success criteria literacy workshop	Large group	1

DATE	DESCRIPTION OF LEARNING ACTIVITY	HOW (PLC TIME, LARGE GROUP, EARLY RELEASE, ETC.)	OUTCOME LIST
Nov. (Week 4)	Guided groups and the use of learning intentions/success criteria math workshop	Large group	1
Dec./ Jan./ Feb.	Read *Challenging Learning Through Feedback* and complete Activities	PLC	2
Dec. (Week 1)	Advisement strategies and share	Large group	3
Dec. (Week 2)	Collaborative learning use of learning intention/ success criteria math workshop	Large group	1
Dec. (Week 3)	Collaborative learning use of learning intention/ success criteria literacy workshop	Large group	1
Jan. (Week 2)	Review look fors and revise	Large group	1–3
Jan. (Week 3)	Independent work use of learning intention/ success criteria math workshop	Large group	1
Jan. (Week 4)	Independent work use of learning intention/ success criteria literacy workshop	Large group	1

At this point in the school year, it would be critical to review data (achievement, implementation, and walkthrough) and determine the direction of the professional development plan for the remainder of the school year. The principal along with their leadership team should have analytical conversations and determine if the first two action steps were meeting the implementation goals. If the outcome is "yes," then moving on to the second action step as a building would be the direction of a large group PD (universal). If, however, the data and implementation indicated that less than 80% of the staff were implementing with fidelity, it would be appropriate to revisit the first action step and "dive in" to the components of the workshop. School improvement plans are often written for more than one year, so allowing the part (PLC) to move forward while addressing the needs of the whole (large group) is a means to an end.

APPENDIX C
Developing Look Fors Protocol

The purpose of this protocol is to engage all staff in developing look fors. Having all staff collaborate and share their understanding helps to define the look fors in a way that doesn't leave a lot of unanswered questions. This protocol will help staff create shared meaning.

Time Required: Typically, this can occur over the course of two meetings. The first meeting lasting 60–90 minutes and the second 45–60 minutes. However, time will vary based on how familiar staff are with content that is being defined.

FIRST MEETING

Step One: Individual Quick Write

Staff members individually write 5–7 statements that answer the question, "What would this strategy (i.e., formative assessment, higher-order thinking, productive groupwork, etc.) look like and sound like in our classrooms and school?"

Step Two: Small Group Share

Once individual lists are developed, staff move into small groups and share lists, identifying common look fors and categorizing them into three different areas: teacher behaviors, student behaviors, and environment. Each look for from the team's consolidated lists is written on individual sticky notes.

Step Three: Categorize Into Three Lists

Sticky notes are gathered and posted under the corresponding category: teacher behaviors, student behaviors, and environment. Staff are divided into three teams (or six depending on the size of the faculty) and asked to review one of the three categories, narrowing the list so that each category has 5–7 look fors.

Step Four: Gather Input

Staff carousel around the room reviewing lists, posing questions, and adding to for clarity. When teams get back to the poster where they started, a debrief is conducted. Questions are addressed during the large group discussion and look fors are revised.

SECOND MEETING

The lists generated during the first meeting are gathered and reviewed by the leadership team for minor editing prior to the second meeting.

During the second meeting, the edited lists are shared, staff review in small groups, and questions are answered to help ensure clarity and clear up misconceptions. At the end of this meeting, you have the school's look for list.

APPENDIX D

Building Capacity Self-Assessment

			WHAT DO I NEED TO DO TO MOVE CLOSER TO BLOOMING?
Overview	**Knowledge**	I understand the importance of connecting the processes of school improvement (mission and vision, data, the plan, professional development, and supervision) and continually work toward alignment.	
		I am clear about the difference between supervision and evaluation.	
		I understand how actionable feedback is necessary to drive my school improvement plan.	
		I realize that formative and summative measures are needed to provide a complete picture of a teacher's performance.	
	Skills	A clear and focused school improvement plan (limited goals and clear language) has been developed collaboratively with staff.	
		All staff are able to articulate the goals and strategies in the school improvement plan.	

			WHAT DO I NEED TO DO TO MOVE CLOSER TO BLOOMING?
Overview	Follow Through	I have developed and am using a clear system in place for how I organize my days and weeks that allows me to observe teachers and attend PLC meetings.	
		Cycles for observations and feedback have been developed.	
Quadrant I	Knowledge	I understand the professional development staff needs in order to enact strategies in the school improvement plan. This is evidenced by a list of professional learning staff outcomes for the year and a detailed plan for achieving them.	
		I understand the benefits of large-group, small-group, and individual learning and have organized professional learning to provide opportunities for all three.	
	Skills	Look fors were developed in collaboration with all staff and are used to provide feedback to staff.	
		I connect the school improvement plan to the work in the other quadrants.	
		Feedback includes a rationale (the why) for the practices that were validated.	
	Follow Through	I share weekly feedback with staff that validates the look fors observed during general walkthroughs. Feedback describes what was observed and why it is important in helping students succeed.	
		I have a method for documenting feedback so I can frequently review to look for patterns and trends across the school.	

(*Continued*)

			WHAT DO I NEED TO DO TO MOVE CLOSER TO BLOOMING?
Quadrant II	Knowledge	I understand that for teachers to think metacognitively about what and how they are teaching professional learning needs to include both content and process learning.	
		I have studied PLCs and what makes them work and what makes them fail. I revisit this information on a regular basis.	
		I understand the importance of, and how to use, student work during collaboration.	
		I continue to develop my own knowledge so I can provide relevant and meaningful feedback to teachers.	
	Skills	When I note differences between PLCs, I adjust learning to meet the group's specific needs.	
		I use a focused walkthrough to help get a deeper sense of the issues that surface during observations or team meetings so I can help support teachers.	
		I have a structure for PLCs that includes identifying clear outcomes and uses a recursive action planning process.	
		I provide teams and individuals with feedback that leads to action.	
		I connect the focused walkthrough to the work in the other quadrants.	

			WHAT DO I NEED TO DO TO MOVE CLOSER TO BLOOMING?
Quadrant II	Follow Through	I make attending and participating in PLCs a priority and rarely miss.	
		Our teams make decisions based on student evidence.	
		I have developed tools to organize feedback and monitor progress.	
Quadrant III	Knowledge	I understand that quality implementation is more than just a compilation of practices. It requires educators to wrestle with what works and why.	
		I embrace the importance of transparency and share all implementation study data with all staff so we can engage in rich dialogue.	
		I realize the need to compile and analyze both impact (student achievement) and implementation data in order to make sound decisions.	
	Skills	I use protocols when sharing data to help ensure all staff voices are heard.	
		I work with teachers to analyze data and make revisions to professional development that support the growth and development of all teachers.	
		I can have meaningful conversations around the implications of the implementation study.	

(Continued)

(Continued)

			WHAT DO I NEED TO DO TO MOVE CLOSER TO BLOOMING?
Quadrant III	Follow Through	Skills	I connect implementation studies to the work in the other quadrants.	
			I conduct implementation studies 3 times a year using a checklist based on look fors.	
			I revise and adapt based on the needs of the staff.	
Quadrant IV	Knowledge		I have a deep understanding of my district/state's teaching standards.	
			I am aware of the need to use various coaching stances during supervisory conversations.	
			I understand the four types of feedback and when each is most effective.	
	Skills		I connect formative observations and feedback to the summative evaluation.	
			I connect the district evaluation system to the work in the other quadrants.	
			I plan for supervisory conferences and have a structure in place for conducting them.	

Quadrant IV	Follow Through	I developed an infrastructure that supports ongoing data collection for individual teachers and staff.	
		I have tools to analyze teachers' current levels of performance.	

REFERENCES

Baker, A., & Bruner, B. (2021). *Integrating evaluative capacity into organizational practice.* Cambridge, MA: Bruner Foundation. Retrieved from http://www.evaluativethinking.org/docs/Integ_Eval_Capacity_Final.pdf

Bambrick-Santoyo, P. (2012). *Leverage leadership: A practical guide to building exceptional schools.* San Francisco, CA: Jossey-Bass.

Bandura, A. (1997). *Self-efficacy: The exercise of control.* New York, NY: W.H. Freeman and Company.

Brookhart, S. M. (2016). *How to make decisions with different kinds of student assessment data.* Alexandria, VA: ASCD.

Brophy, J. (1983). Research on the self-fulfilling prophecy and teacher expectations. *Journal of Educational Psychology, 76,* 236–247.

Bryk, A. S., Sebring, P. B., Allensworth, E., Luppescu, S., & Easton, J. Q. (2010). *Organizing schools for improvement.* Chicago, IL: University of Chicago Press.

Campitelli, G., & Gobet, F. (2011). Deliberate practice: Necessary but not sufficient. *Current Directions in Psychological Science, 20,* 280–285.

Carroll, J. B. (1963). A model of school learning. *Teachers College Record, 64,* 723–733.

Clinton, J. (2021). I am an evaluator of my impact on teacher/student learning. In J. Hattie & R. Smith (Eds.), *Ten mindframes for leaders: The visible learning approach to school success.* Thousand Oaks, CA: Corwin.

Coburn, C. (2003). Rethinking scale: Moving beyond numbers to deep and lasting change. *Educational Researcher, 32*(6), 3–12.

Costa, A. L., & Garmston, R. J. (2016). *Cognitive coaching: Developing self-directed leaders and learners,* (3rd ed.). Lanham, MD: Rowman & Littlefield.

Darling-Hammond, L. (1998). Teacher learning that supports student learning. *Educational Leadership, 55*(5), 6–11.

Daskal, L. (2016, February 9). Six mantras that will set you apart as a leader. *Inc.* Retrieved from https://www.inc.com/lolly-daskal/6-smart-mantras-that-will-set-you-apart-as-a-leader.html

Dewitt, P. (2021). I give and help students/teachers understand feedback and I interpret and act on feedback given to me. In J. Hattie & R. Smith (Eds.), *Ten mindframes for leaders: The visible learning approach to school success.* Thousand Oaks, CA: Corwin.

Donohoo, J. (2017). *Collective efficacy: How educators' beliefs impact student learning.* Thousand Oaks, CA: Corwin.

Donohoo, J. (2021). I collaborate with my peers and my teachers about my conceptions of progress and impact. In J. Hattie & R. Smith (Eds.), *Ten mindframes for leaders: The visible learning approach to school success.* Thousand Oaks, CA: Corwin.

Donohoo, J., & Katz, S. (2020). *Quality implementation: Leveraging collective efficacy to make "what works" actually work.* Thousand Oaks, CA: Corwin.

Donohoo, J., & Mausbach, A. (2021). Moving Beyond Collaboration: The power of joint work. *Educational Leadership, 78*(5), 22–26.

Dufour, R. (2007). Professional learning communities: A bandwagon, an idea worth considering, or our best hope for high levels of learning? *Middle School Journal, 39*(1), 4–8. Retrieved from https://files .eric.ed.gov/fulltext/EJ775771.pdf

Elmore, R. F. (2004). *School reform from the inside out*. Cambridge, MA: Harvard Education Press.

Elmore, R. F. (2008). Leadership as the practice of improvement. In B. Pont, D. Nusche, & D. Hopkins (Eds.), *Improving school leadership volume 2: Case studies on system leadership* (2nd ed., pp. 21–25)., 2nd Ed. Paris: Organisation for Economic Co-Operation and Development.

Fisher, D., Frey, N., Almarode, J., Flories, K., & Nagel, D. (2020). *PLC+: Better decisions and greater impact by design*. Thousand Oaks, CA: Corwin Publishing.

Fullan, M. (2009). *Motion leadership: The skinny on becoming change savvy*. Thousand Oaks, CA: Corwin.

Fullan, M. (2014). *The principal: Three keys to maximizing impact*. Hoboken, NJ: Jossey-Bass.

Fullan, M. (2019). *Nuance: Why some leaders succeed and others fail*. Thousand Oaks, CA: Corwin.

Fullan, M., Hill, P., & Crevlola, C. (2006). *Breakthrough*. Thousand Oaks, CA: Corwin.

Fullan, M., & Quinn, J. (2016). *Coherence: The right drivers in action for schools, districts, and systems*. Thousand Oaks, CA: Corwin.

Gallimore, R., Emerling, B., Saunders, W., & Goldenberg, C. (2009). Moving the learning of teaching closer to practice: Teacher education implications of school-based inquiry teams. *Elementary School Journal. The Chicago Press Journals, 109*(5), 537–553.

Goddard, R., Hoy, W., & Woolfolk Hoy, A. (2004). Collective efficacy beliefs: Theoretical developments, empirical evidence, and future directions. *American Educational Research Association, 33*(3), 3–13.

Goldhammer, R. (1969). *Clinical supervision: Special methods for the supervision of teachers*. New York, NY: Holt, Reinhard & Winston.

Greene, R. W. (2014). *Lost at school: Why our kids with behavioral challenges are falling through the cracks and how we can help them*. New York, NY: Scribner.

Hall, G., & Hord, S. (2006). *Implementing change: Patterns, principles, and potholes* (2nd ed.). New York, NY: Pearson Education.

Hargreaves, A., & Fullan, M. (2012). *Professional capital: Transforming teaching in every school*. New York, NY: Teachers College Press.

Hattie, J. (2009). *Visible learning: A synthesis of over 800 meta-analyses relating to achievement*. New York, NY: Routledge.

Hattie, J. (2015). *What works best in education: The politics of collective expertise*. London: Pearson.

Hattie, J. (2019). *Visible Learning: 250+ influences on student achievement*. Thousand Oaks, CA: Corwin.

Hattie, J., & Smith, R. (2021). *Ten mindframes for leaders*. Thousand Oaks, CA: Corwin.

Hattie, J., & Timperley, H. (2007). The power of feedback. *Review of Educational Research, 77*(1), 81–112.

Hughes, E. (2015). *The Little Gardener*. London, England: Flying Eye Books.

Johnson, S. (2012). The impact of collaborative structure on perceived collective efficacy (Doctoral dissertation). Retrieved from ERIC (ED549482).

Joyce, B., & Showers, B. (1980). Improving inservice training: The messages of research. *Educational Leadership, 37*(5), 379–385.

Katz, S., Dack, L., & Malloy, J. (2018). *The intelligent, responsive leader*. Thousand Oaks, CA: Corwin.

Katz, S., Earl, L., & Ben Jaafar, S. (2009). *Building and connecting learning communities: The power of networks for school improvement*. Thousand Oaks, CA: Corwin.

Leithwood, K., Day, C., Sammons, P., Harris, A., & Hopkins, D. (2006). *Seven strong claims about successful school leadership*. Nottingham, England: National College for School Leadership/ Department of Education and Skills, Nottingham.

Little, J. W. (1990). The persistence of privacy: Autonomy and initiative in teacher's professional relations. *Teachers College Record, 91*(4), 509–536.

Love, N. (2001). *Using data/getting results: A practice guide for school improvement in mathematics and science.* Norwood, MA: Christopher-Gordon Publishers.

MacDonald, E. (2013). *The skillful team leader: A resource for overcoming hurdles to professional learning for student achievement.* Thousand Oaks, CA: Corwin.

Marshall, K. (2013). *Rethinking teacher supervision and evaluation: How to work smart, build collaboration, and close the achievement gap* (2nd ed.). Hoboken, NJ: Jossey-Bass.

Marzano, R. (2003). *What works in schools: Translating research into action.* Alexandria, VA: ASCD.

Marzano, R., Pickering, D., & Pollock, J. E. (2001). *Classroom instruction that works: Research-based strategies for increasing student achievement.* Alexandria, VA: ASCD.

Mausbach, A., & Morrison, K. (2016). *School leadership through the seasons: A guide to staying focused and getting results all year.* New York, NY: Routledge.

Mooney, N., & Mausbach, A. (2008). *Align the design: A blueprint for school improvement.* Alexandria, VA: ASCD.

Newmann, F. M., Smith, B., Allensworth, E., & Bryk, A. S., (2001). Instructional program coherence: What it is and why it should guide school improvement policy. *Educational Evaluation and Policy Analysis, 23*(4), 297–321.

Nottingham, J., & Nottingham, J. (2017). *Challenging learning through feedback: How to get the type, tone and quality of feedback right every time.* Thousand Oaks, CA: Corwin.

Pearson, P. D., & Gallagher, G. (1983). The gradual release of responsibility model of instruction. *Contemporary Educational Psychology, 8,* 112–123.

Pink, D. (2009). Drive: *The surprising truth about what motivates us.* New York, NY: Riverhead Books.

Reeves, D. (2008). *Reframing teacher leadership to improve your school.* Alexandria, VA: ASCD.

Robinson, V. (2011). *Student-centered leadership.* Hoboken, NJ: Jossey-Bass.

Robinson, V. (2018). *Reduce chance to increase improvement.* Thousand Oaks, CA: Corwin.

Ross, J., Hogaboam-Gray A., & Gray, P. (2004). Prior student achievement, collaborative school processes, and collective teacher efficacy. *Leadership and Policy in Schools, 3*(3), 163–188.

Senge, P. (2006). *The fifth discipline: The art and practice of the learning organization.* New York, NY: Doubleday.

Sinek, S. (2015). Lecture: Leaders eat last: Why some teams come together and others don't [Video]. Retrieved from http://www.sai-iowa.org/leaders-eat-last-book-study.cfm

Smith, D., Frey N., Pumpian, I., & Fisher, D. (2017). *Building Equity: Policies and practices to empower all learners.* Alexandria, VA: ASCD.

Sweeney, D., & Mausbach, A. (2018). *Leading student-centered coaching: Building principal and coach partnerships.* Thousand Oaks, CA: Corwin.

Timperley, H. (2011). *Realizing the power of professional learning.* New York, NY: McGraw Hill.

Tschannen-Moran, M., & Hoy, W. K. (2000). A multidisciplinary analysis of the nature, meaning, and measurement of trust. *Review of Educational Research, 70*(4), 547–593.

INDEX

Leadership That Makes an Impact

MICHAEL FULLAN & MARY JEAN GALLAGHER

With the goal of transforming the culture of learning to develop greater equity, excellence, and student well-being, this book will help you liberate the system and maintain focus.

PETER M. DEWITT

This step-by-step how-to guide presents the six driving forces of instructional leadership within a multistage model for implementation, delivering lasting improvement through small collaborative changes.

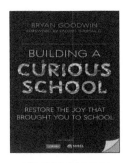

BRYAN GOODWIN

If you've ever wondered anything, really—just out of curiosity—then you have what it takes to lead your school to restored curiosity and your students to well-being and success.

JOHN HATTIE & RAYMOND L. SMITH

Based on the most current Visible Learning® research with contributions from education thought leaders around the world, this book includes practical ideas for leaders to implement high-impact strategies to strengthen entire school cultures and advocate for all students.

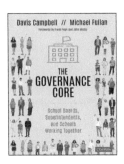

DAVIS CAMPBELL & MICHAEL FULLAN

The model outlined in this book develops a systems approach to governing local schools collaboratively to become exemplars of highly effective decision-making, leadership, and action.

MICHAEL FULLAN, JOANNE QUINN, & JOANNE MCEACHEN

The comprehensive strategy of deep learning incorporates practical tools and processes to engage educational stakeholders in new partnerships, mobilize whole-system change, and transform learning for all students.

JOANNE QUINN, JOANNE MCEACHEN, MICHAEL FULLAN, MAG GARDNER, & MAX DRUMMY

Dive into deep learning with this hands-on guide to creating learning experiences that give purpose, unleash student potential, and transform not only learning, but life itself.

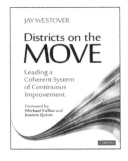

JAY WESTOVER

The transformative framework outlined in this book creates a districtwide approach for changing the culture of learning and creating a coherent system of continuous improvement.

ANTHONY KIM, KEARA MASCARENAZ, & KAWAI LAI

This guide provides battle-tested practices to help leaders build better habits for team learning, meetings, and projects, to achieve a more responsive, innovative organization.

EVAN ROBB

Build the foundations of effective leadership despite daily distractions. Learn how to intentionally use ten-minute opportunities to consider and execute your vision.

AMY TEPPER & PATRICK FLYNN

Nineteen strategies help leaders, coaches, and teachers improve their ability to identify desired outcomes, recognize learning in action, collect relevant evidence, and develop effective feedback.

JULIE M. WILSON

Learn to make sense of challenging change journeys and accelerate implementation with this practical framework that includes human-centered tools, resources, and mini case studies.

GRANT LICHTMAN

Our rapidly evolving world is dramatically impacting how we view schools. *Thrive* shows educators how they can help their schools not only survive but thrive during rapid change.

ERIC SHENINGER

The future-forward framework in this book prepares leaders to harness the power of innovative ideas and digital strategies to create relevant, engaging, and intuitive school cultures.

CHRISTINE MASON, PAUL LIABENOW, & MELISSA PATSCHKE

Envision and enact transformative change with an iterative visioning process, thought-provoking vignettes, case studies from exemplary schools, key strategies and tools, and practical implementation ideas.

KIRSTEN RICHERT, JEFFREY IKLER, & MARGARET ZACCHEI

Shifting empowers educational change leaders to proactively and coherently navigate complex, unprecedented change in schools and establish a school culture in which changemakers can thrive.

A SAGE Publishing Company

Helping educators make the greatest impact

CORWIN HAS ONE MISSION: to enhance education through intentional professional learning.

We build long-term relationships with our authors, educators, clients, and associations who partner with us to develop and continuously improve the best evidence-based practices that establish and support lifelong learning.